Monetarism Under Thatcher

Monetarism Under Thatcher

Lessons for the Future

Gordon T. Pepper
Honorary Visiting Professor, City University Business School

and

Michael J. Oliver
Associate Professor of Economic, Bates College, Maine, USA

In association with The Institute of Economic Affairs

Edward Elgar
Cheltenham, UK • Northampton, MA, USA

Published by
Edward Elgar Publishing Limited
Glensanda House
Montpellier Parade
Cheltenham
Glos GL50 1UA
UK

Edward Elgar Publishing, Inc.
136 West Street
Suite 202
Northampton
Massachusetts 01060
USA

ISBN 0–255–36492–X
Printed and bound in Great Britain by MPG Books Ltd, Bodmin, Cornwall

Contents

Figures and tables

FIGURES

TABLES

The authors

GORDON T. PEPPER, CBE, is an Honorary Visiting Professor in the Department of Banking and Finance at City University Business School. He is a member of the Shadow Monetary Policy Committee and of the Council of Economic Advisers to the Opposition Front Bench. He is also Chairman of Lombard Street Research Ltd.

Professor Pepper was educated at Repton School and Trinity College Cambridge, where he graduated in mathematics and economics.

In 1960 he was the joint founder of the gilt-edged business of W. Greenwell & Co. and revolutionized statistical techniques in the gilt-edged market. For many years he was regarded as the leading commentator on the UK gilt-edged market. In 1972 he introduced W. Greenwell & Co.'s *Monetary Bulletin*, which became one of the most widely read monetary economic publications produced in the United Kingdom in the 1970s and 1980s.

Professor Pepper is a Fellow of the Institute of Actuaries and of the Society of Investment Professionals. He was a Member of the ESRC from 1989–93, Chairman of the Macroeconomic Consortium from 1991–94 and a Member of the Advisory Committee Department of Applied Economics, Cambridge University, 1992–97.

For the IEA he has previously written: *Too Much Money ...?* (with Geoffrey E. Wood; Hobart Paper No. 68, 1976); *A Firm Foundation for Monetary Policy* (IEA Inquiry No. 8, 1989); a short paper, 'Monetary Control, Past, Present and Future', in *The State of the Economy* (IEA Readings No. 31, 1990); *Money, Credit and Inflation* (Research Monograph No. 44, 1990); *Restoring Credibility: Monetary Policy Now* (Current Controversies No. 1, 1992); and *Inside Thatcher's Monetarist Revolution (*published jointly with Macmillan, 1998). He is also the author of *Money, Credit and Asset Prices* (Macmillan, 1994). Professor Pepper is also co-author with Dr Oliver of an article for the journal *Economic Affairs* entitled 'Monetary Targets: An Unfinished Experiment' (1999).

MICHAEL J. OLIVER (www.bates.edu/acad/depts/econ/faculty/oliver/homepage) is currently the Phillips Lecturer in Economics at Bates College, Maine.

Oliver graduated in economic history at the University of Leicester and was awarded his PhD in economics and economic history from Manchester Metropolitan University. He has held posts at the Universities of the West of England, Leeds and Sunderland and has been a Visiting Professor at Gettysburg College, Pennsylvania.

He is the author of *Whatever Happened To Monetarism? Economic Policy-making and Social Learning in the United Kingdom Since 1979* (Ashgate, 1997); *Exchange Rate Regimes in the Twentieth Century* (with Derek Aldcroft; 1st edn, Edward Elgar, 1998) and *Trade Unions and the Economy: 1870–2000* (with Derek Aldcroft; Ashgate, 2000). He has contributed articles to *Twentieth Century British History*, *Economic Affairs*, *Contemporary British History*, *Economic Review* and *Essays in Economic and Business History*.

Foreword

Professor David Laidler

When Jacob Viner wished to express disapproval of the Federal Reserve Board's policies in the early years of the Great Depression, he could find no worse an insult than to say that the Board was displaying '... an attitude towards its functions resembling with almost miraculous closeness that of the Bank of England during its worst period' (Viner 1932: 28). The period Viner had in mind was not, of course, the 1970s, but the years immediately preceding 1810, when the House of Commons' Bullion Committee heard opinions from the Bank's directors that Walter Bagehot (1873) later termed 'almost classical by their nonsense'. As readers of this provocative book by Pepper and Oliver will soon discover, however, some things had not changed very much by the final third of the twentieth century.

The problem in 1810, 1932, the 1970s and 1980s, and in many other episodes too (not least that currently playing itself out in Japan), has been the 'needs of trade', sometimes called the 'real bills' doctrine. This has it that the central bank should be what Pepper and Oliver call a 'lender of first resort' to the financial system, and provide it at all times with an elastic supply of liquidity so that actors in the real economy can have reliable access to whatever amounts of money and credit they need to get on with their everyday business. This pernicious idea also implies that a central bank can do no more than this, and if something untoward should nevertheless happen in the economy, this would only go to show that there are limits to monetary policy's powers.

Now some things have changed, and for the better too, between 1810 and the present. Bank of England doctrine during the French Wars really did have it that the rate of discount made no difference to the economy's demand for loans, and no one has made this absurd claim for a long time. Nowadays indeed, manipulation of the short-term rate of interest is at the very heart of the Bank's policy framework, as it is in most modern central banks. In 1810, moreover, the Bank had portrayed itself as an innocent and powerless bystander as far as inflation was concerned, while nowadays the inflation rate is its explicit and sole policy target. Even the monetary horror stories of the 1970s, when a policy regime that concentrated on output and employment goals, with half an eye cocked at the costs of mortgage finance, was freed to do its inflationary worst after the removal of the exchange rate constraint, are therefore becoming a distant memory.

So why should any busy student of the current British monetary system care if Pepper and Oliver rake up the 1970s and 1980s again, and draw lessons from that experience for reform now, when that system seems to be working rather well? There are, I think, two reasons. First, the policies of those years brought about an extraordinary, albeit often painful, transition in the fortunes of the British economy, and their history is inherently interesting. Second, an account of that history is Pepper and Oliver's chosen way of revealing to their readers what they believe to be a dangerous flaw still remaining in Britain's monetary policy regime. One does not have to accept every detail of their analysis to believe that its overall thrust is compelling and worth further serious discussion.

A brief foreword is no place to engage in a long commentary on the history that Pepper and Oliver deal with. Suffice it to remind the reader that, in the early 1970s, the very idea that inflation was largely a result of past monetary policy, and required monetary measures to cure it, was controversial in Britain. Indeed, it is my distinct recollection that, in 1975, the editors of the *Economic Journal*, being concerned about the length of the article 'Inflation – a Survey' that Michael Parkin and I had prepared for them, suggested that the section of it dealing with the quantity theory of money be omitted on the grounds that this material was largely irrelevant to the applied economics of inflation. If, only a few years later, the group who administered a monetary cure for British inflation contained more sceptics and opportunists than people who actually believed in the treatment and understood how it was supposed to work, that is hardly to be wondered at. But in monetary policy, the devil is all too often in the details, and because those in charge did not understand those details, they got them wrong. As Pepper and Oliver show, this goes quite a way to explaining why monetary policy in the 1980s was so ill-executed and clumsy. And, I cannot resist noting, it underlines the central political irony of the period: namely that the baleful effects on the economy of the switch from a domestic goal to the unsustainable policy of shadowing the Deutschmark ended up doing more damage to Margaret Thatcher's career than to anyone else's, precisely because her scepticism about that exchange rate policy had helped to isolate her politically in the first place.

But interesting though the history it recounts is, this book's important message is for the present. Pepper and Oliver argue that one detail mishandled in the 1980s was the role of the monetary base in the policy regime, and that the Bank of England still has not got this right. Specifically, they suggest that the behaviour of the broad monetary base should become a policy target. As they recognize, this proposal is a hard sell. In my view, this is not just because a battle over it was fought and lost nearly two decades ago, and left very few people with any interest in reviving it. Probably more important, it is apparent that inflation targeting has served Britain very well over the last few years and, as a consequence, there is much to be said for applying the old adage 'if it isn't broken, don't fix it' to the current policy regime.

Let me remark in passing that, in making this optimistic assessment, I am well aware of recent problems in certain sectors of British manufacturing. Let me also, however, express the opinion that these are largely a manifestation of a long-term shift in the balance of comparative advantage away from what is now called the 'old economy'. They should not be laid at the door of a strong pound; and if sterling should depreciate in the near future, either as a result of market forces or as the outcome of policies designed to facilitate its replacement by the euro, these distressed sectors will find themselves in trouble from domestic cost pressures instead.

Be that as it may, if Britain retains a national currency, I would not advocate *replacing* inflation targets with targets for the monetary base. Monetary policy needs to be firmly anchored in expectations of low and stable inflation if it is to succeed, and the expectations in question are those of the public at large, not just of financial markets. That public has not got the faintest idea what the monetary base is, but it does know about inflation, so policy explicitly aimed at the latter can attain a degree of credibility that can never attach to one based solely on a monetary aggregate. That is one of the things we have learned in the 1980s and 1990s. But I am all for giving a monetary aggregate a prominent supporting role in the policy regime, and I am not willing to argue with Pepper and Oliver's contention that, in the case of Britain, the base is the right one, without a lot more thought and analysis.

Even a dyed-in-the-wool monetarist such as myself, however, has to admit that monetary policy – anchored by a credible inflation target, and implemented by manipulating short-term interest rates while allowing money growth to evolve as a consequence of interactions among the central bank, financial institutions and the public, works well most of the time. To put it in Pepper and Oliver's terms, I believe that, even when money growth targets are given a role, setting interest rates in order to achieve them by influencing the demand for money is always a flawed policy, but I also believe that, quite often, it doesn't do any harm; and the same goes for regimes in which money growth targets are regarded as superfluous altogether.

But 'quite often' is not 'always'. Consider the current plight of Japan. Confronted with a chronically pessimistic non-bank public that is very unwilling to borrow, the Bank of Japan seems to have concluded that lowering short term interest rates to zero exhausts the policy measures open to it. But an institution with a monetarist concern for the behaviour of monetary aggregates would not have given up at this point. It would also have indulged in large-scale open-market operations in longer-term securities, not to mention unsterilised intervention in the foreign exchange market, but the Bank of Japan has tried neither. Like the Federal Reserve system in the early 1930s, it has been meeting all the needs of trade for money and credit at very low interest rates, but also like the Federal Reserve system, it seems to have forgotten that, by expanding the monetary aggregates sufficiently, it can also significantly influence those needs.

This sorry record from abroad should give British readers no comfort, however. Things are going well right now, but the Bank of England's monetary policy is still based on a version of the needs-of-trade doctrine. To be sure, this version gives a central role to short-term interest rates and is therefore a great deal less dangerous than that of 1810. But if something were to come unstuck in Britain to depress business expectations, as it did in Japan, the Bank of England would have to improvise its response, and there is no reason to believe that it would do better than its Japanese counterpart. There is no policy device in place that would automatically lead to the right corrective measures. A monetary base target would be one such possibility, and as Pepper and Oliver also show, it would help with many other less dramatic eventualities too. As they say, however, its introduction would necessarily change important aspects of the day-to-day implementation of policy, so it would be best done when things are quiet, at the very time, in fact, when it is not urgently needed.

The present is just such a time, and therefore an excellent time to start discussing such proposals. I commend this book to anyone interested in the current conduct of monetary policy in Britain.

David Laidler
Bank of Monreal Professor, University of Western Ontario
Canadian Bankers' Association Fellow, C.D. Howe Institute

Preface

Professor Colin Robinson

Professor Gordon Pepper's work on monetary policy is well known to readers of IEA publications who will recall, in particular, his *Money, Credit and Inflation*[i], which was one of the Institute's best-sellers. In *Monetarism Under Thatcher: Lessons for the Future*, he has collaborated with Michael Oliver, an economic historian who has written on the history of monetary policy,[ii] to produce a book which not only analyses that history – as seen by practitioner and historian – but draws policy conclusions from Britain's experience.

This new book complements Gordon Pepper's *Inside Thatcher's Monetarist Revolution*[iii] to provide novel and controversial insights into how monetary policy was formed by politicians and officials, many of whom either did not fully understand or did not believe in monetary control; to reveal the views of the main protagonists; and to explain why the authors conclude that there is a serious flaw in Britain; s present monetary policy regime.

Gordon Pepper was an influential figure in the City in the days when the foundations of monetary control were being laid. He knew all the key players and he was an adviser to Margaret Thatcher during those critical years. His inside knowledge and analysis have, in this book, been combined successfully with Michael Oliver's ability to sift, put into context and present important material about British economic history.

In Part III the authors turn their attention to how to provide a 'stable framework for monetary policy', drawing on their experience and their analysis of history. They argue that the wide monetary base should be controlled but with no mandatory ratio for bank reserves. There would be a pre-announced target for the monetary base which would reduce uncertainty, de-politicize monetary policy and allow interest rates to be set by market forces. Control would be achieved '... at a lower level of interest rates than under the present system in the UK'.

All IEA publications contain the views of their authors, not those of the Institute (which has no corporate view), its Trustees, Advisers or Directors. But the careful analysis and considered policy conclusions of this book –

especially about the virtues of monetary base control – deserve to be examined seriously by the monetary authorities and the Government.

Colin Robinson
Professor of Economics, University of Surrey
Editorial Director, Institute of Economic Affairs

NOTES

i IEA Research Monograph 44, Second Impression, 1991.
ii *Whatever Happened to Monetarism? Economic Policy-making and Social Learning in the United Kingdom Since 1979*, Ashgate, 1997.
iii *Inside Thatcher's Monetarist Revolution*, Macmillan in association with the Institute of Economic Affairs, 1998.

Acknowledgements

The authors owe a special debt to Sir Alan Walters for encouragement and many suggestions. They would also like to thank the following for kindly reading parts of the text and offering valuable suggestions for improvements: Professor Derek Aldcroft (Manchester Metropolitan University); Professor Roger E. Backhouse (University of Birmingham); Sir George Blunden; Professor Neil H. Buchanan (University of Wisconsin-Milwaukee); Professor Forrest Capie (City University Business School); Dr David Cobham (University of St Andrews); Professor Tim Congdon (Lombard Street Research); Lord Howe of Abervon; Lord Lawson of Blaby; Peter Lilly, MP; Sir Adam Ridley; Professor Michael Smith (University of South Carolina); Andrew Smithers; Lady Thatcher; and Professor Geoffrey E. Wood (City University Business School). We are also grateful for the comments of two anonymous IEA referees. Any remaining errors of fact, analysis or interpretation are, of course, our own.

Parts of this book have been presented at several academic conferences: the History of Political Economy Conference (Duke University, Durham, NC, 1999); the Economic and Business Historical Conference (San Antonio, TX, 1999); the Fifth Annual European Conference On The History Of Economics (Paris, 1999); and The Thatcher Years: The Rebirth of Liberty (Hofstra University, Hempstead, New York, 2000). The authors would like to thank the participants for their comments and criticisms.

We would like to thank the library staff at Bates College, Durham University, Gettysburg College, University of Kent and the University of Sunderland for their bibliographic help and Jamie Oliver for his technical assistance with the figures.

We would also like to thank PFD on behalf of Lord Lawson of Blaby for permission to reprint extracts from *The View from No. 11* by Nigel Lawson (Copyright © Nigel Lawson, 1992).

Executive summary

Following the Introduction, this book is divided into three Parts. Part I is an historical overview of monetary policy between the 1950s and early 1970s and a more detailed assessment of monetary policy between the mid 1970s and late 1980s. Part II raises the question of what monetary lessons should have been drawn by the authorities over the last thirty years and whether it is in fact possible to provide a stable framework for monetary policy. Part III provides the solution for a stable framework for monetary policy, namely monetary base control (MBC).

INTRODUCTION

The account of monetary policy in this book is not a detached historical one because one of its authors, Pepper, was too involved with the events of the 1980s. Pepper's role was to provide raw material and analysis. Oliver's was to help select the most interesting material, put it into context and maximize its use for historians.

Various types of monetarist are defined:

- A 'genuine monetarist' is someone who believes that the money supply should be controlled, as an intermediate target for controlling money GDP.
- A 'political monetarist' is someone who does not share the belief of a genuine monetarist but is nevertheless in favour of publishing a monetary target to reduce inflationary expectations and to manage expectations in financial markets to stop them from behaving in an undesirable way.
- A 'pragmatic monetarist' is someone who, as time has passed and practical experience has been gained, while still accepting the theory of monetary control, has concluded that the theory cannot be turned into working practice.

Early drafts of either the whole book or the sections concerning them were sent to certain key officials and politicians and to some of their close associates. Meetings or correspondence followed, which became extremely valuable as disagreement was clarified and argument became much tighter. The result was an improvement and, hopefully, enhancement of the authority of this book. It must be stressed that the people involved have not seen the final version of the book and that they have not approved its contents.

PART I

- Peter Middleton, Permanent Secretary of the Treasury from 1983 to 1991, was a political monetarist. This was perhaps the biggest surprise we have uncovered in writing this book. During the early 1980s, Middleton was believed to be an advocate of monetary control as an intermediate target for controlling nominal GDP and not merely of the use of monetary targets for political purposes. A close textual analysis of his 1988 NIESR Jubilee Lecture, supported by a recent interview, reveals that the authorities were not following a money supply policy but were merely managing expectations. He was a political monetarist and not a pragmatic monetarist.
- Geoffrey Howe was Chancellor of the Exchequer from May 1979 to June 1983. His strength was that he was determined that the UK should adopt voluntarily the sort of policy that the IMF had imposed in 1976. He did not however possess the technical qualifications to choose between the different measures of money and the different forms of control offered to him. Dell has argued that Howe's monetarism looked like Treasury policy (Dell 1996: 454 and 468). We know from Middleton that this policy was political monetarism. Howe's failure to scrap the constraint on the growth of banks' interest-bearing-eligible liabilities (IBELs), the 'corset', when he abolished exchange controls (which had been distorting the published data for the money supply downward), suggests strongly that he gave priority to trying to hit the published targets and influence expectations rather than control underlying monetary growth. Our conclusion is that he became, perhaps unwittingly, a political monetarist.
- Nigel Lawson, Chancellor of the Exchequer from June 1983 to October 1989, has drawn our attention to his statement about his views that he considers crucial: 'It is perfectly sensible to target the money supply in some countries and at some times, and to target the exchange rate at others' (Lawson 1992: 421). He describes the choice between a monetary or foreign exchange rate target as being a second-order decision (Lawson 1992: 420). He defines an exchange rate target as a form of monetarism (Lawson 1992: 419 and 421). Lawson was not therefore a monetarist as defined either in this book or by no less an authority than Milton Friedman. He clearly gave priority to the politics of targets.

- Prime Minister Margaret Thatcher was a genuine monetarist, more by conviction than scientific argument, but who nevertheless always believed that price stability could best be achieved by controlling the money supply.
- The overall conclusion of Part I is that, in spite of the instinct of the Prime Minister, the authorities never attempted to control the *supply* of money, by controlling the reserve base of the banking system, as the North American and Swiss schools of monetarism argued they should, and that they only paid lip service to controlling the *demand* for money, although they did attempt some control over the counterparts of broad money. The experiment in the 1980s was mainly an exercise in political monetarism.

PART II

After examining the history of monetary policy in the UK since Radcliffe and establishing that the UK authorities did not implement genuine monetarism in the 1980s, we raise the question of what monetary lessons should have been drawn by the authorities over the last thirty years and whether it is in fact possible to provide a stable framework for monetary policy. In Part II, some of the themes of Part I are developed and the focus is on the lessons that were *not* learnt from the experience of the 1970s, the 1980s and the 1990s. There are four main arguments:

- First, that the UK authorities consistently paid insufficient attention to the behaviour of bank lending to the private sector and failed to comprehend the significance of what was happening when it was known that bank lending had become either very buoyant or, conversely, sluggish. The authorities made the mistake committed by most non-monetary economists who focus on the economic decision associated with a credit transaction and ignore the impact of the additional money created by the credit transaction, which may be called 'fountain-pen money'. *The credit effect is a one-off. The monetary effect continues.* If buoyant growth of credit persists, the monetary effect compounds. Fountain-pen money created by buoyant bank lending was an important cause of the Barber boom in the early 1970s and the main cause of the Lawson boom in the late 1980s.
- Secondly, it is possible to offset the excessive growth of fountain-pen money in the short run by 'overfunding'; that is, by selling more gilt-edged stock than is needed to cover the public sector net cash requirement. We severely criticize Lawson's decision in 1985 to suspend overfund-

ing and find the recent action to separate debt management from monetary policy, with the setting up of the new Debt Management Office, bizarre.

- Thirdly, that the authorities' current 'one club' policy of relying solely on changes in short-term interest rates to control the growth of nominal GDP is foolhardy.
- Fourthly, that control of bank lending badly needs strengthening. We acknowledge the importance of overfunding to offset excessive growth of fountain-pen money, but this is only a short-term solution and one that has been made impossible with the separation of debt management from monetary policy. Two other possible methods of control, namely quantitative control on bank lending and capital ratios, are decisively dismissed. The overall conclusion of Part II is that the only solution that stands up to further examination is control of bank reserves; that is, monetary base control (MBC).

PART III

Part III provides our solution for a stable framework for monetary policy. We revisit the essence of monetary base control and the debate about MBC that occurred in the 1980s and the objections towards it that continued to be raised in the 1990s. We make the following arguments:

- The wide monetary base should be controlled but there should not be a mandatory ratio for bank reserves. The wide definition consists of banks' deposits with the Bank of England and their vault cash, plus notes and coin in circulation with the public. With the exception of one small item these comprise the bulk of the Bank's liabilities.
- Advocates of MBC merely argue that the Bank should accept the discipline of controlling the growth of its own balance sheet. Without such a discipline, monetary policy will not be based on a firm foundation. If its balance sheet is growing too quickly the Bank should sell some assets, for example a bill in the domestic money market or foreign currency in the foreign exchange market; it should buy assets if its balance sheet is growing too slowly.
- The Bank should, accordingly, decide on the quantity of bills (and repos) in which it deals each day in the money market instead of dealing in whatever quantity of bills the banks want (albeit it at a price of the Bank's own choosing). In other words the Bank should cease to be lender of first resort. Short-term interest rates should be determined by market forces instead of being administered by the Bank.

- MBC would stop unsustainable growth of banks' balance sheets and would prevent the conditions in which financial crises tend to occur. If a crisis does occur in spite of this, lender-of-last-resort operations by the Bank should have complete priority over MBC.
- MBC would prevent progressive departures of the money stock from target rather than precise short-term control.
- One advantage of a monetary target is that it de-politicizes monetary policy. The wide monetary base is the best aggregate to target because it is the one least prone to artificial manufacture.
- A pre-announced target for the monetary base would eliminate the uncertainties created by the monetary authorities. The markets would *know* that the monetary base would increase by a certain percentage each day. Because interest rates would be determined by market forces and not set by the authorities, the days of central bank watching would be well and truly over.
- There are several other advantages of MBC. Interest rates being set by market forces should make sure that rates are not changed by too little, too late, as has happened so often in the past. MBC would exert some direct influence on bank lending. Automatic sales of debt, similar to overfunding or underfunding by the Bank, would occur to offset the behaviour of bank lending. Pressure would be spread across markets and assets, and asset allocation would be determined by normal market criteria instead of being administered by officials.
- The controversial assertion in this book is that an increase in the price of money – that is, in interest rates – combined with a constraint on the availability of supply has a larger effect than an increase in interest rates in isolation. If this is correct MBC is not merely a system of monetary control that would stand up to pressure but control would also be achieved at a lower level of interest rates than under the present system in the UK.
- Our unequivocal conclusion is that, if the UK does not become a member of the European Single Currency, the debate about monetary base control should be reopened.

Introduction

The advent and the abandonment of monetarism in the UK has fuelled many articles and books in the last twenty years, each seeking to bring a new insight to a period of widespread change in monetary policy. Among the many reasons for the fascination of this period, three above all have kept the debate alive. The first is that major changes or shifts in macroeconomic policy are rare and thus the attempt to apply monetarism in the UK has drawn much attention from economists and economic historians. Secondly, the period witnessed a considerable blurring between the roles of the key players in economic policy making, namely politicians, officials, academics, think tanks and the media. The interaction between politicians and officials is particularly piquant during the Thatcher era, as is the importance of the politician in the economic policy-making process. Finally, there is still a question mark over the exact legitimacy of the so-called British 'monetarist experiment'; specifically the extent to which the period between 1979 and 1985 can qualify to be labelled monetarist in any economic sense of the word.

By way of background, it should be recalled that during the early 1970s there were a number of widespread reforms to the operation of UK monetary policy. By the mid 1970s, monetary policy in the form of targets for monetary aggregates had become a major element of macroeconomic policy. This emphasis marked an important shift away from Keynesian economic thinking towards monetarism. The validity of the arguments for monetarism gained increasing acceptance in the media, the City and eventually the Conservative Party. Unlike the Conservative Party, however, the Labour Government which had originally adopted money supply targets did not accept the underlying intellectual premise of monetarism. After winning the Election in May 1979, the Conservatives came to power with the intention of conducting economic policy along monetarist lines. However, within six years their initial strategy for monetary policy had been abandoned.

Given the existing literature of this period, it might seem strange to present yet another account of monetarism in the 1980s. The problems with writing contemporary history are legion, particularly when the subject is one of the most controversial episodes in twentieth-century British monetary history. Some economic historians would find it difficult to accept that now is the time for a reappraisal of monetarism under Thatcher, while the majority of historians have proceeded cautiously with the existing primary material since the early 1970s, preferring to wait before more documents are available under the thirty year rule. Where they have become involved, the majority of economic historians have not been concerned with exploring the issues of policy transformation, thereby returning the more technical issues to their counterparts in economics (cf. Middleton 1998, 2000; Oliver 1997). If the debate is now too historical for the economists but not historical enough for the historians, this leaves a lacuna in the Thatcher literature which is not easy to breach.

We would agree with Peter Clarke's recent comments that even though the thirty year rule prevents the release of official documents from the Public Record Office, there is little point in economic historians imposing their own thirty year rule and not commenting on the post-1979 period, especially when so much rich source material exists (Clarke 1999: 301).[1] Furthermore, we believe that we bring a new insight into the period between 1975 and 1990 that is not contingent on the release of official papers. Concomitantly, some of the material we present in this book – together with the copies of correspondence which we hold with many of the leading actors of this period – should be considered raw material for future historians.

As we have indicated, the so-called British 'monetarist experiment' has generated a vast amount of ink and an enormous amount of controversy. Before the publication of this book, the following assessment of the controversy was probably typical of any that could be found in the economics literature:

> Amongst supporters and opponents alike, there was a general air of expectancy and a feeling that this experience would answer important theoretical questions about the design of macroeconomic policy.
>
> In the event, the experiment has proved, or rather disproved nothing. Monetarists have denied that an experiment ever took place; they have developed new theories to explain the behaviour of the income velocity of circulation or blamed external shocks for structural shifts in the demand for money and the natural rate of unemployment. Non-monetarists, in contrast, have interpreted the Government's failure to execute its strategy as planned as evidence that the money supply cannot be controlled; the gyrations in the velocity of circulation have been taken as further proof that the demand for money is inherently unstable and the coincidence of mass unemployment and stable inflation has been used to attack the nature rate hypothesis.
>
> In a political sense, the 1979–82 experiment certainly did provide a test of practical monetarism and, if nothing else, it established that rigid monetary rules are not the panacea for inflation-free growth in a dynamic, open economy that the Government originally hoped. But in the economic sense of testing key macroeconomic theories, the experiment has merely served to illustrate once again the limitations of empiricism and to highlight the fact that the sources of controversy in economics run far deeper than many of its practitioners would like to believe. (Healey 1987: 496)

This book will show that this type of summary is far too simplistic for the historian of contemporary economic policy making to accept at face value, aside from the fact that it can be challenged on economic grounds.[2] The crucial point is that many economists remain deeply sceptical of monetarism and do not hesitate to provide evidence which shows that in the early 1980s the money supply was not controlled. We do not wish to dispute these findings; indeed, we argue that it is precisely because of this that monetarism is unfinished business. Moreover, despite the huge literature of academic econometric work and the heated debates between monetarists and their detractors, there is no evidence to prove that monetarism was rejected in the UK because of the strength or weakness of a particular regression. Clearly there is more to this debate than econometric tests and, even if economists are able to evaluate particular decisions and outcomes from a technical perspective, they are able to explain very little about the process of economic change; how and why economic policies change course and who is instrumental in the policy shifts.

Our first reason for wanting to reopen the debate on monetarism under Thatcher was to attempt to bridge the gap between economists and historians, and to argue that the existing literature has reached an intellectual cul-de-sac. There has been a widespread misunderstanding about the nature and extent of monetarism under Thatcher by both groups of academics and no thorough investigation into the extent to which Milton Friedman's monetarism was applied in the British context, or how monetarist theory was modified in the light of its application in Britain. We believe that both economists and economic historians have to come to terms with the fact that Keynesian policies in 1981 would have been disastrous. This applies especially to the 364 of them who were the authors of an infamous letter to *The Times* shortly after that year's budget, which included no less than 76 professors and 5 out of the 6 surviving ex-chief economic advisers to the Treasury. Of equal concern to us is that much of the discussion on the Conservatives' monetarist strategy has become unfocused because the economic terminology has been far from clear, and to address this we felt that it was important to employ tight working definitions of monetarism from the outset of our research which allow us to contextualize the British experiment afresh.

The second reason for writing this book is to draw attention to the role of the most important players in the British monetarist controversy and to explore what happened to the mindset of these players during the 1980s. We argue that the explanation for the abandonment of monetarism can be found in examining the contribution of several key actors. We seek to ascertain whether the commitment to monetarism of these actors was either genuine or ephemeral by analysing written accounts published during and after the period and, wherever possible, conducting interviews and entering into private correspondence. The individual protagonists that we focus on include Peter Middleton (Permanent Secretary of the Treasury), Geoffrey Howe and Nigel Lawson (Chancellors of the Exchequer) and Margaret Thatcher (Prime Minister). We also examine the role of a key institution, namely the Bank of England.

Our third reason was that we wished to explain what went wrong in the UK economy after the Thatcher Government abandoned monetarism. This enables us to focus on the failure to control bank lending and to include a more detailed discussion on funding policy than has been published since the mid 1980s (Bank of England 1984). The evidence of failure allows us to advance the case for the introduction of the one untried method of monetary control in the United Kingdom, namely monetary base control. Thus, to the economists who feel that the arguments over money supply targets and funding policy are only unfinished business to economic historians, we would point out that many of the lessons of the post-1975 period have yet to be drawn by policy makers and are especially pertinent for monetary economists in the twenty-first century.

Two caveats need to be sounded from the outset. First, this book is about monetary policy and not a history of macroeconomic policy making during the Thatcher years, covering, for example, the demise of Keynesian economics and the rise and fall of the New Cambridge Policy Group. Second, parts of the book are not a detached account, because one of its authors, Pepper, was too involved with the events of the 1980s and has been the UK's leading advocate of monetary base control for over thirty years.

As will be explained, Peter Middleton, who was Permanent Secretary of the Treasury from 1983 to 1991, in the conclusions of his NIESR Jubilee Lecture in 1988, entitled 'Economic Policy Making in the Treasury in the Post-War Period', stated: 'the main effort must be directed towards maintaining the credibility and reputation of macro economic policy so that financial markets behave in a way which generally supports it' (Middleton 1989: 51). Throughout the late 1970s and early 1980s Pepper was the leading analyst in the gilt-edged market and was often described in the media as a guru. As such, he was one of the main targets when the authorities were attempting to manage expectations. Pepper's other involvements were:

- He was an unofficial adviser to Margaret Thatcher when she was Leader of the Opposition.[3]
- He attended the seminar in the Treasury, when Howe was Chancellor, before the Conservative Government announced its Medium-Term Financial Strategy (MTFS) (Howe 1994: 155).
- From January 1988 he was one of the Group of Outside Independent Economists (Gooies) that Lawson set up when he was Chancellor (Lawson 1992: 389).
- He maintained close contact with Alan Walters when the latter was Chief Economic Adviser to the Prime Minister, Margaret Thatcher (Pepper 1998: 179).

Pepper's involvement, and therefore his provision of raw material, ceased when John Major became Chancellor of the Exchequer (October 1989). This is why the historical account in this book finishes in the late 1980s.

Despite these caveats, both authors have attempted to establish balance in Part I by providing an historical overview of monetary policy between the 1950s and early 1970s before turning to a more detailed assessment of monetary policy since the mid 1970s. The more contemporary chapters that explore monetarism under Margaret Thatcher have been written with the intention of providing raw material and historical insights for use by historians. Pepper's role was to provide the material. Oliver's was to help select the most interesting material, put it into context and maximize its use for historians. The material used included a selection from the various primary and secondary sources that are available. Early drafts of either the whole book or the sections concerning them were sent to the principal actors, for example to Lawson, and to certain close associates of the actors. The authors' aim was to try to make sure that they had not misrepresented the views of the actors. Meetings or correspondence followed. This became extremely valuable as disagreement was clarified and argument became much tighter. Much of the text of the book had to be rewritten. The result was improvement and, hopefully, enhancement of the authority of the book. The authors would like to thank all of those involved. *It must be stressed that the actors have not seen the final version of the book and that they have not approved its contents.*

DEFINITIONS EMPLOYED IN THIS BOOK

'Genuine Monetarists', 'Political Monetarists' and 'Pragmatic Monetarists'

As we outlined above, one of the improvements that we wished to make on the existing literature was more accurate descriptions of the various types of monetarist. A 'genuine monetarist' is defined in this book as someone who believes that inflation is essentially a monetary phenomenon and that excessive monetary growth, which persists, leads in due course to a rise in inflation. Genuine monetarists stress that the time lag before this happens is long and variable. It follows that knowledge is insufficient to fine tune the money supply – that is, to boost it in an attempt to minimize a recession and curtail its growth to minimize a boom – and that the best policy is to aim at steady monetary growth. Expressed differently, genuine monetarists advocate that the money supply should be controlled as an intermediate target for controlling nominal GDP.

Some economists and politicians are in favour of publishing monetary targets although they do not accept the argument for controlling the money supply as an intermediate target for controlling nominal GDP. Their reasons for wanting to publish targets are to reduce inflationary expectations and to manage expectations in financial markets to stop them from behaving in an undesirable way. Some may also have a hidden agenda. For example, an associated target for the public sector net cash requirement (PSNCR) helps the Bank to argue with the Treasury that fiscal policy should be tightened. It also strengthens a Treasury minister's hand when he or she is arguing with a minister in charge of an expenditure department that public expenditure must be curtailed. An announced discipline can also help a government to resist pressure to ease policy from, for example, 'wets' in the Cabinet and backbench members of parliament. Those who are in favour of monetary targets but who do not accept the argument that the money supply should be controlled as an intermediate target for controlling nominal GDP may be called 'political monetarists'.

Most genuine monetarists agree with political monetarists that targets for the money supply should be published in the hope that this will reduce inflationary expectations. If so, the composition of nominal GDP will be less inflation and more real growth. The importance that genuine monetarists attach to influencing expectations depends in turn on the importance that they attach to rational expectations theory. Some expect the effect to be substantial whereas others are less optimistic.[4] *When monetary data become distorted there can be a conflict between managing expectations and controlling underlying monetary growth. The crucial question at such times is whether to give priority to the former or the latter. Monetarists who give priority to managing expectations come close to being political monetarists.* Whichever way priority is given it should be noted that the rhetoric of political monetarists and genuine monetarists who attach importance to rational expectations theory is almost identical. It is easy to confuse the two. But genuine monetarists who give priority to controlling underlying monetary growth are fundamentally different.

There is yet another group of economists. In the words of Sir George Blunden (Deputy Governor of the Bank of England 1986–90) by the end of Howe's chancellorship some of the original converts to monetarism had become disbelievers. But others – many others – had moved to still accepting the theory of monetary control but believing that the theory could not be turned into working practice. They had found it quite impossible to find which measure of the money supply to target, at what level any target should be set to provide the desired economic results and how to achieve the target when it had been set.[5] This group of economists may be called 'pragmatic monetarists'. (The response to pragmatic monetarists is given at the end of Chapter 11.)

This book does not dwell at length on the distinctions between genuine monetarists who concentrate on the behaviour of narrow money (M0 as an *indicator* and M1), for example Professor Patrick Minford, and those who concentrate on broad money (M3 or M4), for example Professor Tim Congdon; nor does it provide a historiography of this debate. For a discussion of the former, in particular of Congdon's and Minford's positions, see Pepper 1998: Part III.

Ways of Controlling the Money Supply

Three ways of controlling the money supply are identified in this book. First, the North American and Swiss schools of monetarism argue that the stock of money in the economy should be regulated by the central bank controlling the *supply* of money and that this should be done by controlling the reserve base of the banking system; that is, monetary base control. Secondly, the money stock can be controlled by changing the price of money (that is, interest rates) to alter people's *demand* for money. The third method of control is for the authorities to operate on the so-called 'counterparts' of broad money, for example the public sector net cash requirement (the old public sector borrowing requirement (PSBR)) and sales of public sector debt to the non-bank private sector. The third method, which is peculiar to the UK, is best considered as a supplement to demand-side control.

PART I

History

1. A brief history of monetary policy since Radcliffe

For much of the post-war period, British economic policy was characterized by a fixed exchange rate, restricted international capital mobility and Keynesian (demand) management. In this environment, fiscal policy was favoured as the main way to achieve full employment and this was only bolstered by the investigation of the Radcliffe Committee that sought to diminish the importance of the quantity theory of money (HM Treasury 1959). By the 1960s, however, a variety of problems had emerged in the operation of monetary policy, and both domestic and international developments led to a revival of the quantity theory.

'PRE-COMPETITION AND CREDIT CONTROL'

The investigation by the Radcliffe Committee into the operation of UK monetary policy was very influential and dominated the mindset of most economists, advisers and politicians into the 1970s.

The suggestion of the Committee was that monetary policy should be responsible for the external balance while fiscal policy should be assigned the task of maintaining domestic balance. In practice, the role of monetary policy was not absolutely clear; it was used as a supplementary tool of demand management to 'back up' fiscal policy and as a means of protecting the exchange rate through high interest rates in the recurrent balance of payments crises throughout the period.

In essence, the Committee:

- argued that monetary policy should be responsible for the external balance and should play a secondary role to fiscal policy in the context of demand management;
- stated that monetary measures acted on the level of demand through altering the liquidity position of the public and hence its investment decisions;
- emphasised the significance of liquidity but did not clearly define its meaning;

- was unimpressed by the Bank of England's (the Bank) measures to smooth movements in gilt-edged prices;
- recognised the distorting effects of quantitative controls and recommended that the authorities should not rely on restrictions on bank lending or on hire purchase regulations for long periods of time.

Developments during the 1960s, however, showed how the views of the Committee were based more on the 'stop–go' cycles of the 1950s than the persistent balance of payments problems of the 1960s. The realities of demand management were not as smooth in practice as the authorities had hoped, and while demand was crudely encouraged by fiscal stimulation, the subsequent overheating was solved by a tightening of monetary policy to cure the deficit on the balance of payments. Due to the deleterious state of the balance of payments after 1964, the economy was subjected to frequent deflationary policies and an increasing reliance was placed on monetary policy as a measure to check external flows by fluctuations in short-term interest rates. On the domestic side, monetary policy was a supplementary tool to 'back up' fiscal policy, mainly through restricting credit to borrowers.

The Radcliffe Committee had been concerned about the problem of excess liquidity in the banking system, which resulted in the liquidity ratio of the clearing banks being in excess of the conventional minimum of 30 per cent (Dimsdale 1991: 115). During the 1960s, little progress was made in reducing the liquid assets ratio of the banking system because of the expansion of holdings of commercial and other bills and of money at call with the discount market. The discount market also increased the size of its commercial bill portfolio. Within the banking sector as a whole, liquid assets became increasingly composed of private rather than public debt.

The restrictions on bank lending encouraged bill finance by companies which provided the banks with additional liquid assets – the Bank responded by restricting commercial bill holdings in 1965. It was clear from this development that the numerous restrictions on the banking system coupled to the weakening of control through the liquid assets ratio pointed to a need to redefine reserve ratios and to review the techniques of control.

The Bank was also concerned about the problems arising from the management of long-term debt. In the 1950s and 1960s there had been three aims of debt management: first, to maximize investors' desire to hold gilt-edged stock in the long run; secondly, to assist the aims of monetary policy; and thirdly, to minimize the cost of servicing the National Debt. In practice priority was given to the first because the Bank was worried about what might happen when the large wartime and nationalization issues came up for redemption. The chosen tactic was 'to preserve of an orderly market', as it was considered that investors would be encouraged to hold more stock if they were confident that they would always be able to sell stock close to the prevailing middle market price. The result was that the Bank supported the gilt-edged market when it was falling and stopped it from rising too quickly when it was firm.

As the authorities were primarily concerned with the problems of debt management, they did not exercise control over the money supply. By intervening in the bond market to underpin security prices, the Bank was expanding the liquidity of the banking system. Banks were encouraged to sell gilt-edged securities when they wanted to increase their advances and to respond to calls for special deposits by reducing holdings of gilts rather than loans to the private sector. Clearly, the authorities did not recognize the connection between the financial markets: when the Bank Rate was raised to strengthen the reserves, there was a tendency for gilt price to fall; by intervening in the gilt market the Bank encouraged sales of gilts and the outward movement of funds, depleting the reserves. The whole process of trying to strengthen the reserves was thus a zero sum game.

'COMPETITION AND CREDIT CONTROL' – MARK I

Competition and Credit Control (CCC) was introduced in 1971 and was designed to encourage competition between the clearing banks for new business while ending the existing distortions in the financial system which had favoured the development of secondary banking. Qualitative and quantitative controls were abandoned, the new system of control extended a reserve asset ratio to all banks and the power to call special deposits was retained. The Bank also stopped supporting the gilt-edged market.[6] The spirit of CCC reflected a preference for indirect rather than direct government control and a belief in market forces. As such it was a decisive shift away from the subdued attitude towards competition in the money markets which had existed since the 1930s.

At an academic seminar at the launch of CCC, the Research Director of the Bank, Kit McMahon, explained that the quantitative controls on bank lending had caused progressively greater distortions.[7] At first, the non-clearing banks had gained at the expense of the clearing banks. After the controls were extended to the non-clearing banks, fringe banks (such as the London and County Bank) gained at the expense of fully authorized banks. McMahon stated that the distortions had reached the point at which controls had to be scrapped and expressed the hope that there would be no need for further controls for a few years.

It is important to rectify one popular misconception. The combination of reserve asset ratios combined with the power to call for special deposits suggested that the Bank intended to control the reserve base of the banking system. This was not the case. Measures were designed merely to increase the Bank's control over interest rates. If the system was being squeezed, it was thought that the banks would sell assets and that these could be bought by the Bank at prices of its own choosing. Subsequent accusations that the left hand of the Bank was doing the opposite to its right hand (the one instituting the squeeze and the other undoing it) missed the point, as this was always intended. But note that things were not quite what they appeared to be.

With the introduction of CCC and the freeing of the pound in 1972, two big constraints on monetary policy had been abolished within a very short time and these were reinforced by the relaxation of controls on commercial rents and property development. Thus while the aim of increased competition was achieved, the sweeping away of controls released a pent-up demand for credit and a reservoir of supply to meet the demand. The result was a credit explosion.

Four things should be noted. First, Prime Minister Edward Heath would not agree to a rise in the Bank Rate. As a result, banks' base rates were held down.

Secondly, when the banks began to feel pressure on their reserves in 1972, they did not sell assets as expected but bid for additional funds, such as certificates of deposit (CDs) and wholesale deposits, which they could use to make loans and to acquire reserve assets. This move away from 'asset management' to 'liability management' had not been foreseen in CCC.

Thirdly, the discount market was used to manufacture reserve assets. At its simplest, a bank issued a CD and used the funds to increase its call money with a discount house, the call money qualifying as a reserve asset for the bank, while the discount house used the call money obtained from the bank to purchase the CD issued by the bank.[8]

Fourthly, with base rates held down and CD rates rising, arbitrageurs could make money borrowing from a bank and investing the proceeds in CDs. Such 'round tripping' inflated the data for both bank lending and broad money. This was the first of the major distortions to the money supply that were to come.

The outcome was that broad money grew by 22 per cent in both 1972 and 1973. In nominal terms the increase over the two years was £15,414m. The main explanation was the lax credit policy rather than an easing of fiscal policy when Anthony Barber was the Chancellor of the Exchequer. Banks' and building societies' sterling lending rose by no less than £11,482m (numerically, 74 per cent of the rise in broad money) over the period while the public sector net cash requirement (then called the public sector borrowing requirement or PSBR) amounted to £6,043m. Even allowing for distortions to data due to 'round tripping' broad money gave a very clear indication of the awful rise in inflation that was to follow. The Heath Government subsequently fell from power.

The definitions of the various monetary aggregates are given in Appendix 1. A complication is that not only has attention been focused at different times on different definitions of broad money (M3, sterling M3 and M4), because for example building societies have become more similar to banks, but the definition of an aggregate has also sometimes changed. For ease of reading, the terms 'narrow money' and 'broad money' have been used in this book. For preciseness and where appropriate, the actual aggregate to which reference is being made is given in brackets. The above data are in fact for M4 and M4 lending, source Bank of England (1998: tables 2.2 and 6.1).

'COMPETITION AND CREDIT CONTROL' – MARK II

The Bank had earlier but belatedly responded to the credit explosion. In December 1973 a constraint on the growth of each bank's interest-bearing-eligible liabilities (IBELs), officially known as the supplementary special deposit scheme but colloquially known as the 'corset', had been introduced to stop banks bidding for funds. Competition between banks was restrained once again, although this time the constraint was on their liabilities rather than their assets.

The corset became effective in April 1974 and had little impact because bank lending soon subsided of its own accord in the face of the 1974/5 recession, a collapse in asset prices, and with both bankers and borrowers becoming cautious after having observed the pain from bad debts. Bank and building society lending was sluggish (M4 lending grew by an average of only £88m a quarter between the middle of 1974 and the end of 1975). It did not become buoyant again until the second quarter of 1976.

The corset was reactivated twice. The first occasion was announced in November 1976, after a sterling crisis forced the UK to borrow from the IMF, and was effective from February to August 1977. The second, announced in June 1978, was prompted by a buyers' strike in the gilt-edged market and was effective from August 1978 until June 1980.[9] By 1978, however, many bankers had learnt how to avoid the constraint. All a bank had to do was to persuade a customer to issue a commercial bill rather than draw down on a line of credit. It could then arrange for the commercial bill to be 'accepted' by an acceptance house, after which it would qualify as a primary liquid asset and the bill could then be sold to someone instead of a CD. The result was that the borrower received funds and the investor obtained a highly liquid asset without broad money (sterling M3) being increased. This was known as the 'bill leak'. The result was that data for broad money were distorted downward. This was the second major distortion. Was this one deliberate?

2. Monetarism in the UK

THE MOVE TO MONETARY TARGETS

Monetarism received a great deal of attention in the mid 1970s, from politicians, officials in the Bank and the Treasury, academics and the media, partly because the published data for broad money had been a superb indicator of the awful rise in inflation at the time. Economists in the Bank carried out a series of investigations examining both the Keynesian and monetarist arguments. Demand for money equations for both narrow and broad money were estimated and thought to be sufficiently reliable for policy purposes. The Bank started having unpublished 'aims' for broad money (M3) that were used for internal purposes and which were hit with reasonable success.

With the money supply apparently under control why was there an economic crisis at the end of 1976?

As already stated, bank lending remained sluggish until the second quarter of 1976. This offset an increase in the public sector net cash requirement (PSNCR) and was the main reason why broad money behaved in accordance with the Bank's 'aims' until then. As the recession ended bank lending recovered. Between the end of March and the end of September lending by banks and building societies (M4 lending) grew at an annual rate of over 16 per cent. The offset had disappeared. At first broad money did not reflect this buoyancy, because money had started to pour abroad.

This brings us to the IMF's favourite monetary aggregate, which is domestic credit expansion (DCE). The IMF chooses DCE rather than the growth of broad money as a target because a balance of payments deficit reduces the latter. At its simplest a government can raise funds to finance excessive public expenditure by selling its foreign exchange reserves. The IMF obviously does not want this to happen.[10] More generally, if the domestic supply of money in a country exceeds the domestic demand for money some of the excess will tend to flow out of the country. Technically in the UK, external and foreign currency financing of the public and banking sectors, one of M4's so-called 'counterparts', turns negative (the 'counterparts' of broad money are explained in Chapter 7).

Chancellor Denis Healey claimed in the middle of 1976 that there was no economic justification for the fall in sterling. Unfortunately he focused on the behaviour of broad money and not on DCE. The warning of trouble to come came in June 1976 when published data showed that DCE during the three months to mid May was running at 23 per cent, expressed as a percentage of the stock of broad money (sterling M3) and as an annual rate (Greenwell 1976). A severe sterling crisis followed in October 1976, with the UK being forced to borrow from the IMF and accept its conditions, one of which was a constraint on DCE.

Monetary targets were published for the first time in the UK in 1976, just before the negotiations with the IMF after the sterling crisis. There is no doubt that the subsequent imposition of the target for DCE by the IMF and the favourable response of the economy to the IMF's measures gave monetary targeting in the UK a boost. A simple story would be that this led directly to the annual targets for broad money which became an essential part of the Conservative Government's subsequent Medium Term Financial Strategy, and which were eventually suspended in 1985. The story is not, however, so straightforward, as this book will show.

CONTROLLING THE MONEY STOCK

There are three ways of trying to ensure stable monetary growth. The North American and Swiss schools of monetarism argue that the stock of money in the economy should be regulated by the central bank controlling the *supply* of money and that this should be done by controlling the reserve base of the banking system. This is described in Part III and, for the moment, can be called supply-side control.

As we will discuss later in this book, most economists in the UK do not accept the argument for controlling the monetary base. It must be emphasized, especially for US readers, that historically the monetary system in the UK has been, and continues to be, very different from that in the US and from the descriptions in many textbooks. The Bank of England makes no attempt at all to control the quantity of bank reserves. As already explained, the reserve asset ratio and power to call for special deposits under Competition and Credit Control were designed merely to reinforce the Bank's control over interest rates and were not intended to control the reserve base of the banking system.

Such a device to increase the Bank's control over interest rates was not new. An earlier one was the way in which the weekly Treasury bill issue used to be underwritten by discount houses. The reason for this that was usually advanced was to ensure that the government received all the funds that it needed. Discount houses were indeed given valuable privileges in return for incurring the underwriting obligation. This explanation was, however, phoney. The true one was more complicated. The tender for Treasury bills was on a Friday (that is when the price of the issue and hence the Treasury bill rate – that is, the discount rate – was established) but the actual issue of bills was spread over the following week. The size of each issue was deliberately pitched greater than the Exchequer's predicted requirement for finance. This was done to ensure that the discount market required assistance from the Bank nearly every day. Iron control over interest rates was thus maintained because the assistance was always given at a rate of interest of the Bank's own choosing. Underwriting the Treasury bill issue was a charade to reinforce the Bank's control over interest rates.[11]

It should be stressed that the Bank was and remains an openly declared and unlimited lender of first resort, albeit at a price of its own choosing. This is illustrated by the definition of a 'primary liquid asset' under Competition and Credit Control. These were assets that the Bank was willing, at all times and in all circumstances, to purchase (again at prices of its own choosing). Since 1981 the UK has not had any reserve requirements for banks. Appendix 3 elaborates on the differences between the UK and the US monetary systems.

Instead of controlling bank reserves the Bank operates through changing interest rates; that is, through the price of money. This leads to the argument that, if the money stock is to be controlled, people's *demand* for money should be controlled by altering interest rates.

In more detail the procedure for demand-side control is:

- Prepare an economic forecast (that is probably based on a large macroeconomic model of the economy, which may be largely Keynesian).
- Predict people's demand for money, using the demand for money equations that have been derived, at the level of interest rates assumed in the macroeconomic model.
- If the resulting demand for money is inconsistent with the target for the money stock, calculate the rate of interest that will bring the demand for money into line with the target.
- Alter interest rates accordingly.
- Wait for the alteration in rates to have its effect.

There are many things that can go wrong with the above process, for example the initial economic forecast may be wrong or something may happen to the economy during the waiting period.

The third method of monetary control is to operate through the 'counterparts' of broad money. This is explained in Chapter 7. It is a type of supply-side control that is peculiar to the UK.[12] It is best considered as a supplement to demand-side control.

Leaving aside the debate about the mechanism of monetary control, monetary targets can be adopted for two reasons. The first is because the authorities intend to control the money supply as an intermediate target for controlling nominal

GDP, as 'genuine monetarists' advocate. The second is that such targets can, as explained in the Introduction, be used for political purposes, in particular to influence expectations in financial markets in an attempt to stop them from behaving in an undesirable way, as 'political monetarists' advocate. In 1976, a sterling crisis had forced the UK Government to borrow from the IMF and there were examples of buyers' strikes in the gilt-edged market enforcing policy changes. Volatile interest rates, exchange rates and share prices were disrupting the real economy. In an attempt to stop this from happening, monetary targets were introduced to help stabilize expectations in financial markets. Yet to what extent did the officials regard monetarism as a political exercise? Were they genuine, political or pragmatic monetarists?

3. Monetarism and the officials

The historical records of this period can be divided into (1) memoirs of politicians; (2) pronouncements *made at the time* by Treasury ministers, the Governor of the Bank and officials; (3) accounts made by officials after the period had ended; and (4) memoranda, official minutes of meetings, ministerial papers, and so on (collectively known as 'British official papers'). Economic historians are well aware that the purpose for which something has been written should be borne in mind when assessing its contents. The memoirs of politicians may, for example, contain attempts to rewrite history in their favour and need to be rigorously scrutinized. The second of the above categories should be heavily discounted because pronouncements by the Treasury and the Bank are frequently designed to influence confidence in general and expectations in financial markets in particular, and can be deliberately misleading. The third category is more reliable than the first two, although even here officials may be tempted to absolve themselves from blame. The final category is the most reliable and, when supplemented with the other three categories, provides the richest material for historians. Due to the thirty year rule for British official papers it is not at present possible to carry out a much fuller historiography based on primary sources for the post-1970 period. Readers need to be aware that Chapters 3, 4 and 5 are based on a mixture of the first three categories and have been supplemented wherever possible with interviews and written correspondence with politicians and officials.

Towards the end of their period in office the three Permanent Secretaries to the Treasury prior to Terry Burns gave major lectures about managing the economy. In 1968 William Armstrong gave the Stamp Memorial Lecture, in which he described the problems of steering a complex modern economy. In 1978 Douglas Wass gave the Johnian Lecture, entitled 'The Changing Problems of Economic Management' (Wass 1978). In 1988 Peter Middleton gave the NIESR Jubilee Lecture, entitled 'Economic Policy Formulation in the Treasury in the Post-War Period' (Middleton 1989). The conclusions of Middleton's lecture are remarkable. They are given in full below:

> Economic policy is heavily constrained by the nature of the world we live in. Policy-makers have to be sensitive to changes in the environment and ready to adjust their policies as appropriate. With global financial markets *the main effort must be directed towards maintaining the credibility and reputation of macro economic policy so that*

> *financial markets behave in a way which generally supports it.* It is not possible to intervene in financial markets to produce directly the results the government wants.
>
> More generally, the power of governments to influence the economy is limited. Even in the confident days of the 1960s it was more limited than was believed at the time, as the difficulties of the 1970s revealed. The key to good government is to recognise the limits of the government's ability to influence the economy, to resist pressure to do something about problems which government cannot solve, and to make sure that those things for which the government is directly responsible – macro-economic policy, taxation, and the provision of public service – are done as efficiently as possible. (Middleton 1989: 51, emphasis added)

The conclusions have been given in full to illustrate that the highlighted part in italics in the first paragraph, '*the main effort must be directed towards maintaining the credibility and reputation of macro economic policy so that financial markets behave in a way which generally supports it*', is the only really positive and constructive conclusion. There are other conclusions that Middleton might have included in his final paragraphs, which suggests that he attaches great importance to the one he gave. Middleton's conclusion was in fact an extension of the themes in Wass's lecture and a paper, 'Setting Monetary Objectives', given in 1982 by John Fforde, who had just retired having been the Executive Director of the Bank responsible for domestic monetary policy when monetary targets were first adopted, at a conference organized by the Federal Reserve Bank of New York (Fforde 1983).

Wass's lecture described how the real economic relationships on which the old economic models were built had broken down and how the forecasts from those models had ceased to be reliable. It then described the way in which the financial flows between savers and borrowers, both within national economies and between countries, had grown substantially in relation to economic activity. It continued with the way in which the importance of the behaviour of financial markets had grown – about how they had become more volatile – and finally the way in which financial markets had enforced policy changes.

Using rather obscure language, Fforde (1983: 200) distinguished between 'the "political economy" of a money supply *strategy*' and 'the "practical macro-economics" of a money supply *policy*'. He explained that 'the former expression has to do with political presentation to a wide variety of audiences' and the latter was 'concerned with macroeconomic relationships and their stability or instability, for instance, with relationships between the money supply as an intermediate target and the ultimate objectives of policy regarding prices, output and employment'. He explained, 'the practice of intermediate targetary in the United Kingdom was due only in part to its associated and often "monetarist" economics' (Fforde 1983: 201).

In the main body of his lecture Middleton listed the policy changes from the mid 1970s under three categories. He started with two changes in theoretical conventional wisdom at that time: 'First, the ability of changes in fiscal or monetary policy to alter the level of output or employment for more than a temporary period was increasingly questioned. Second, the belief in a long-run trade-off between unemployment and inflation – the Phillips curve – broke down' (Middleton 1989: 48).

Middleton then stated: 'in the minds of markets, and probably also in terms of public perceptions within the UK, the IMF agreement [in 1976] marked a decisive point'. He gave three decisive changes. The first is given below in full; the others are then summarized.

> First, in my view, was the explicit embracing of monetary policy. This enabled us to join those other countries which established monetary targets as a way of imposing financial discipline in a world of floating exchange rates and differential inflation. Monetary targets are intermediate objectives, which enable countries to establish programmes to reduce inflation in line with their own particular circumstances. If further demonstration was needed that things were different, the choice was made in 1977 to stick to the monetary policy by allowing sterling to float upwards – something which would have been impossible five years earlier. *The importance of this episode is nothing to do with textbook monetarism*, though there was quite an industry at the time to work out who was a dedicated monetarist, who was a reluctant monetarist, and who went along with it because markets believed it, although they didn't (the disbelieving monetarist). It was the first step in acknowledging that we really were part of the world system and that we could no longer ignore financial markets or treat them as enemies. We became prepared to espouse what everyone else – both markets and governments – regarded as essential priorities. (Middleton 1989: 48–9, emphasis added)

The second change was the IMF's insistence on ceilings for public borrowing, which enabled the Treasury to implement an effective system of cash control of public expenditure. The third was the principle of setting fiscal and monetary policy objectives for a number of years ahead.

Middleton went on to observe that the MTFS introduced in 1980 gave 'policy a sense of purpose which can be presented with simplicity, coherence and clarity' (Middleton 1989:4) and that it implied 'the intention to eschew measures which might bring short-term benefits but with long-term costs' (Middleton 1989: 49), while 'the medium-term dimension to policy itself added greatly to market credibility and the chances of success' (Middleton 1989: 49). The text stressed that credibility and expectations in financial markets were crucial to policy making in today's world of global markets.

When assessing Middleton's lecture a distinction should be drawn between monetary policy and a policy of controlling the money supply. Neo-Keynesians used to measure the stance of monetary policy by the level of nominal interest rates; that is, without allowing for inflation. Later they changed to measuring the stance by the level of real interest rates. Monetarists, in contrast, argue that the stance should be measured by the behaviour of the monetary aggregates. The explicit embracing of monetary policy mentioned in the third extract from the lecture does not necessarily mean that the authorities were following a money supply policy. Further, the paragraph describes changes in the minds of markets and public perception; that is, it describes what markets and the public think has happened, which is not necessarily the same as what has actually happened. Notice also the remark, '*the importance of this episode is nothing to do with textbook monetarism*' and the references to dedicated, reluctant and disbelieving monetarists.

At this stage of the analysis Middleton appears to have been a political monetarist but this will become clearer as the discussion proceeds.

4. Monetarism under Thatcher

The Conservative Government's experience with monetarism post-1979 is more complex than their Labour predecessors'. The economic policy of the Conservative Party had become increasingly influenced by many of the monetarist and 'supply side' arguments emanating from the United States in the 1970s and, after winning the General Election in May 1979, the Conservatives came to power with the intention of conducting economic policy along monetarist lines. However, the application of theoretical monetarism in the UK was stymied by many practical difficulties and the 'monetarist experiment' was suspended in 1985. While there was a twilight period when there was a target for M0 – which had been introduced alongside the one for sterling M3 in 1984 – monetary targeting was in effect abandoned in March 1987 when the Chancellor of the Exchequer, Nigel Lawson, began to shadow the Deutschmark. Excessive monetary growth was ignored. Inflation then rose, more or less precisely in accordance with monetarist theory. The mystery is why Lawson changed from monetary targeting to managing the exchange rate, especially as the Prime Minister was opposed to the change. To understand this and to fully comprehend the twists and turns of the British monetarist experiment, the story becomes more complicated.

To begin to unravel the story it is instructive to start by considering the state of the monetarist debate in the UK in the early 1980s. Essentially, there were three things happening at this time. First, there was the publication of the Green Paper *Monetary Control* in March 1980 (Bank of England and HM Treasury 1980). Secondly, a few weeks after publication of the Green Paper the Government's Medium Term Financial Strategy (MTFS) was launched (HM Treasury 1980). Thirdly, concurrent to the publication of the MTFS in March 1980, the Treasury and Civil Service Select Committee of the House of Commons, which had been investigating the debate surrounding monetary control, published a report in two volumes (Treasury and Civil Service Committee 1980). Each development will be considered in turn.

THE GREEN PAPER *MONETARY CONTROL*

In contrast to the Labour Party in the 1970s, the Green Paper suggested that the Government intended to control underlying monetary growth and not merely to use monetary targets for political purposes. The following are extracts:

> No single statistical measure of the money supply can be expected fully to encapsulate monetary conditions, and so provide a uniquely correct basis for controlling the complex relationships between monetary growth and prices and nominal incomes. The degree of substitutability between forms of money or liquidity just inside or outside their respective measures means that it is insufficient to rely on one measure alone: in assessing monetary conditions the authorities have to have regard to a range – including not only the narrow measure (M1) but the wider measures of money (M3, sterling M3) and various still wider measures of private sector liquidity ... (Bank of England and HM Treasury 1980: iii)

> As no one aggregate is by itself a sufficient measure of monetary conditions it could be argued that there should be targets for several or all. But this would make it much more difficult for the market and the public to appraise the determination of the authorities to meet their monetary objectives ... (Bank of England and HM Treasury 1980: iv)

> For the present, therefore, the Government intends: –
> (a) to formulate the monetary target in relation to one aggregate;
> (b) to continue to use sterling M3 for this purpose;
> (c) to take into account growth of other aggregates, directing policy to progressive and sustained reduction in the rate of growth of all, although not necessarily by the same amount. (Bank of England and HM Treasury 1980: v)

However, the main body of the Green Paper's text appeared to be more agnostic to monetary control than the introduction. Non-attributable briefings at the time suggested that there was a difference of opinion between the Treasury and the Bank, and that Middleton had written the introduction whereas the Bank had been responsible for the text.

THE MTFS

By the end of the 1970s, there were a number of economists who had suggested a new policy framework for the UK. Tim Congdon, for example, who had reported on the activities of the House of Commons Expenditure Committee in 1974 and 1975 for *The Times*, had seen that the way fiscal policy operated in practice was far removed from the textbook descriptions and became convinced that fine tuning was an illusion. This first-hand experience of crude Keynesian inadequacies had led him to advocate alternative policies (Congdon 1992: 36–7). Congdon also acknowledges an important source of inspiration in his discussions with Terry Burns and Alan Budd at the London Business School. Burns and Budd gave greater academic cohesion to these policies. Equally, Lawson – whose political dexterity would eventually sell the new MTFS to the Conservative Party – was arguing for 'a long term stabilisation programme to defeat inflation, recreate business confidence and provide a favourable climate for economic growth' (Lawson 1978).

The perceived failings of Keynesian economic policy, coupled with the ideas of three economists and one politician, were crucial to the success of the MTFS, while the elevation of Burns to the Government's chief economic adviser in 1980 was important to take the message into the Treasury. The new macroeconomic strategy placed the control of inflation above the commitment to full employment, and central to the MTFS was the emphasis given to controlling the growth of the money supply. The 1980 MTFS was at the opposite extreme to the Radcliffe Report.

In short, the MTFS had four main features by 1980. First, that macroeconomic policy should be conducted within a medium-term perspective. Clearly, this represented a shift from how economic policy was visualized in the 1960s and 1970s. Secondly, there was an identifiable shift from a real to a nominal framework within the MTFS. Thirdly, there was to be a more active use of monetary policy, in particular the elevation of interest rates over direct controls as the main instrument of monetary policy. The authorities were to announce a target aggregate for broad money (sterling M3, as expected) and would raise interest rates if monetary growth appeared excessive. The definition of the money supply target in the 1980 MTFS added the proviso that 'the way in which the money supply is defined for target purposes may need to be adjusted from time to time as circumstances change' as a footnote to Table 5 (HM Treasury 1980: 16). Fourthly, a greater emphasis was placed on controlling the public sector net cash requirement.

Managing Expectations

There was a contrast between the description of the way monetary targets would be operated contained in the introduction to the Green Paper *Monetary Control*, supposedly written by Middleton, and the qualification about the use of the sterling M3 definition contained merely in a footnote in small print in the MTFS. According to a non-attributable briefing the explanation was that two decisions had been taken at this time. The first was to adopt monetary targets and the second was to announce the targets, the objective of the second being to influence expectations. The introduction to the Green Paper had focused on the first and had described how the policy was meant to work in practice, but this was complicated. The MTFS focused on the second and it was thought that the impact on expectations would be maximized by having one simple target that was easy for people to understand. This was why the MTFS had been drafted in the way it had been. This was consistent with the views of genuine monetarists who judged the theory of rational expectations to be important.[13]

Middleton was believed at the time to be an advocate of monetary control as an intermediate target for controlling nominal GDP – that is, a genuine monetarist – and not merely of the use of monetary targets for political purposes – that is, he was not a political monetarist. His career casts some light on what was in fact happening. Between 1969 and 1972 he was Private Secretary to Tony Barber when the latter was Chancellor of the Exchequer. When Barber started to receive bad publicity in the press, he appointed Middleton as the Treasury's press officer. As such, Middleton was most able and became very adept at handling the media. He later rose to become Permanent Secretary, an appointment that is not made without someone being a most efficient operator, including having the ability to manipulate people. From his NIESR Jubilee Lecture there is now no doubt that Middleton attached great importance to influencing expectations in financial markets. The suggestion is that he operated at various different levels and that the introduction to the Green Paper, as well as the MTFS, was designed to influence expectations. More precisely, the latter was designed to influence the relatively uninitiated whereas the former was designed for opinion formers.[14] In the words of an ex-official, 'the Treasury unashamedly managed expectations'.[15] In essence, Middleton was a spin-doctor, a quarter of a century before it became known by this name.

The date of Middleton's spinning should be noted. It was March 1980, which was too soon for someone to have concluded from practical experience that monetary theory could not be turned into working practice. Middleton was not therefore a pragmatic monetarist. The conclusion is that he was a political monetarist all along, which is consistent with his NIESR Jubilee Lecture. Middleton's spinning is an excellent example of the rhetoric of a political monetarist being identical to that of a genuine monetarist who believes in the importance of operating on expectations.

The extent to which the authorities were prepared to go in their attempts to manage expectations is illustrated by the imposition of the corset in the mid 1970s. Recapitulating, under this a bank was penalized if its interest-bearing-eligible liabilities (IBELs) grew too quickly but the penalty was easy to avoid. All a bank had to do was to persuade a borrower to issue a commercial bill instead of drawing down on a line of credit and persuade a depositor to hold a commercial bill rather than a CD. This was the second distortion described earlier. A third one occurred after exchange controls were abolished in October 1979, when it became even easier to circumvent the corset by reclassifying a domestic deposit as a euro sterling deposit and a domestic loan as a euro sterling one. The effect of the corset was artificially to depress data for IBELs and hence broad money (sterling M3), which was the aggregate being targeted. As Anthony Harris once wrote in the *Financial Times*, 'a corset is a device for producing deceptive figures'. Deception was the rule then and it appears that this continued well into the 1980s. The excuse was that it was needed to manage expectations in financial markets and that it was therefore in the 'national interest'.

THE TREASURY AND CIVIL SERVICE SELECT COMMITTEE DEBATE

The Memorandum on Monetary Policy was a cosmopolitan document which sought evidence from North America, Germany, France, Canada and Switzerland. The evidence (both written and oral) taken during the course of the investigations from the distinguished panel of economists, government advisers and politicians contained a range of viewpoints. While it was to be expected that Lord Kaldor would be vehemently hostile to the idea of monetary control, far more surprising was the disagreement among the monetarists over *how* to control the growth of the money supply. While all the monetarists agreed that the money supply needed to be controlled (and that it was important to avoid a specific exchange rate objective), there was a clear division among them between supply-side monetarists who believed in monetary base control and demand-side monetarists who did not.

Milton Friedman did not hide his disapproval of the method of monetary control in the UK when he responded to the Treasury and Civil Service Committee's Questionnaire in 1980:

> I could hardly believe my eyes when I read, in the first paragraph of the summary chapter [of the Green Paper *Monetary Control*], 'the principal means of controlling the growth of the money supply must be fiscal policy – both public expenditure and tax policy – and interest rates'. Interpreted literally, this sentence is simply wrong. Only a Rip Van Winkle, who had not read any of the flood of literature during the past decade and more on the money supply process, could possibly have written that sentence. (Friedman 1980: 57)

Friedman was not impressed with the decision by the authorities to use fiscal policy as a means of influencing interest rates for a given money target: by reducing the PSNCR as a percentage of GDP, the money supply would not grow so quickly and interest rates could be kept low. This characteristic, where fiscal policy was to be made consistent with monetary policy and lose its pre-1979 demand management status, led Friedman to comment that 'there is no necessary relation between the size of the PSBR [as the PSNCR was then called] and monetary growth' (Friedman 1980: 56). (A response to Friedman's comments is given in Appendix 3, which describes the differences between the US and the UK monetary systems, and Chapter 7, which elaborates on the UK's peculiar system of trying to control the 'counterparts' of monetary growth.)

5. Monetarism and the politicians

It would be fair to say that during their discussions with the IMF, the Labour Party's commitment to monetarism was opportunistic. In his memoirs Denis Healey (Chancellor of the Exchequer between March 1974 and May 1979) says that monetary targets were published largely to placate the financial markets and he never accepted Friedman's theories (Healey 1989: 343 and 491). He clearly introduced the targets for political purposes and not as an intermediate target that was seriously intended to control nominal GDP. Healey, in his own terminology, was a 'disbelieving monetarist'. In the terminology of this book, he was an arch political monetarist.

The Conservative Party, on the other hand, had a number of apparently keen proponents of monetarism, including Keith Joseph (Founder of the Centre for Policy Studies and Secretary of State for Industry from May 1979 to September 1981), Geoffrey Howe (Chancellor of the Exchequer from May 1979 to June 1983), Nigel Lawson (Chancellor of the Exchequer from June 1983 to October 1989) and Margaret Thatcher (Prime Minister from May 1979 to November 1990).

KEITH JOSEPH

Keith Joseph was definitely a genuine monetarist. He dated his own conversion to monetarism as April 1974, and his empathy towards the writings of Friedman is expressed clearly in his 1974 Preston speech (Joseph 1977: 4). This speech was the first time that Joseph had publicly championed the monetarist cause, and its contents became the lodestar for the New Conservatism. In the speech Joseph attacked demand management, renounced incomes policies and argued that the expansion of the money supply, by itself, was responsible for inflation. In short, Joseph declared himself happy to be a monetarist. The impact of the speech on the British political debate at the time was considerable, and for many weeks afterwards the letter columns of *The Times* were filled with commentary on Joseph's speech.

It would be quite wrong to suggest that the majority in the Conservative Party shared Joseph's views; most of the Shadow Cabinet were particularly antipathetic to monetarism. Despite gaining the support of Margaret Thatcher, who held the leadership of the Conservative Party from 1975, Joseph did not have a groundswell of support in the Party for his economic views. However, any Tories who thought that the Thatcher–Joseph interest in monetarism was merely a fad were going to be disappointed.

GEOFFREY HOWE

A style of management often employed in the UK is to have a lay chairman of a board whose other members are experts. For example, apart from Leslie O'Brien and Eddie George, Governors of the Bank of England have not been career central bankers. They have usually been prominent merchant or commercial bankers, for example Gordon Richardson from Schroders, the Earl of Cromer from Barings and Robin Leigh-Pemberton (Lord Kingsdown) from Natwest. The lay chairman brings all-round perspective, common sense and judgement to the board. Howe, who is a lawyer rather than an economist, was in this mode at the Treasury.

There is no doubt that Howe had conviction. As a member of the Government in the early 1970s he had learnt from bitter experience what happened when Heath was Prime Minister and a permissive economic policy had been followed. Howe was determined that the UK should adopt voluntarily the sort of policy that the IMF had imposed in 1976.[16] In broad terms he succeeded in doing this. As a result of his determination he can reasonably claim to be the most successful post-war Chancellor (Dell 1996: 487).

The IMF measures included a target for a monetary aggregate, namely domestic credit expansion. Howe chose broad money (sterling M3) instead and there is no doubt that he tried very hard to hit the published targets when he was Chancellor. He recalls with pride that when he left the Treasury in 1983 he was presented with a chart showing the record of how the money aggregates had been within their target bands during 1982–83, countersigned by Peter Middleton, Terry Burns, Eddie George and Alan Walters (Howe 1994: 275). It is not at all clear however that he fully appreciated the distinction between this and controlling underlying monetary growth – that is, monetary growth after allowing for distortions – as an intermediate target for controlling money GDP. The distortions to broad money were greatest during his chancellorship. He inherited the ones from Healey and these became progressively greater as the corset was left in place. Worse still, he did not scrap the corset when he abolished exchange controls in October 1979 but waited until June 1980. During this period circumventing the corset was ridiculously easy, as explained earlier, because banks could classify deposits and loans as eurosterling ones. Unlike the 'bill leak' there was no way of estimating the 'euro leak'. Subsequently Howe completely lost control of the published data for broad money as the previous distortions unwound. (Appendix 2 discusses the behaviour of the monetary aggregates in 1980–81 in some detail.)

Howe states, 'One of the greatest challenges of the Chancellor's job is the extent to which he has to make judgements and reach conclusions about a huge range of technical subtleties ... in the last resort in the name of common sense' (Howe 1994: 172). Howe was not a technical expert. He appears not to have realized that different weights should be placed on different aggregates depending on the circumstances. Dell has described him to be naïve as a monetarist and not to possess the technical qualifications to choose between the different measures of money and the different forms of control offered to him, and that 'his readiness to follow Treasury advice was an example, perhaps, of the Treasury's skill in taking a political slogan and turning it to its own purposes ... Howe's monetarism looked like Treasury policy' (Dell 1996: 454 and 468). We now know from Middleton's NIESR Jubilee Lecture what that policy was. It was political monetarism.

Howe has nevertheless categorized himself as 'an attentive and tenacious student of the still widely divergent theories of monetarism and one of the least unsuccessful practitioners of the art, as a crucial (if frustratingly elusive) component of economic policy.' (Howe 1994: 274)[17] In terms of the definitions of this book, that would make him a pragmatic monetarist. His failure to scrap the corset when he abolished exchange controls suggests strongly that he gave priority to trying to hit the published targets and influence expectations rather than control underlying monetary growth. He became, perhaps unwittingly, a political monetarist.

Further, Howe's commitment to monetary targets was never a genuine long-term one. He discloses in his memoirs that he always hankered for the Exchange Rate Mechanism (ERM) and had consistently advocated that the UK should join ERM 'when the time is right' (Howe 1994: 276). In November 1978 he had told the House of Commons that the Opposition (that is, the Conservatives) was in principle in favour of full membership and there was a commitment to join in the Conservatives' manifesto for the 1979 election (Howe 1994: 111). In October 1979, at a formal meeting with the Prime Minister to discuss ERM when exchange controls were abolished, he argued that ERM should remain a medium-term objective but Margaret Thatcher 'was particularly concerned about the potential conflict between the government's monetary targets and the EMS [European Monetary System] intervention requirements' (Howe 1994: 274). Howe appears to have maintained the same position at another formal meeting with the Prime Minister in January 1982, at which Lord Carrington (Foreign Secretary), Gordon Richardson (Governor of the Bank), Kit McMahon (Deputy Governor of the Bank), Douglas Wass and Alan Walters were also present, when Margaret Thatcher won the argument for staying out for the time being (Howe 1994: 275). Finally Howe states that he judged that 'the time was right' after he had been in the Foreign Office for a little time – that is, from 1983 on, when he was no longer Chancellor of the Exchequer – and 'did so not primarily for foreign policy or for European reasons, but because I had come once again to regard as practical and worthwhile the view which I had originally formed in November 1978' (Howe 1994: 276). Howe, like Lawson (see below), thought of monetary and exchange rate targets as alternatives that were not fundamentally different.

NIGEL LAWSON

Lawson was in many ways the opposite of Howe. He was an economist and not a layman. In spite of what is stated below he was, technically, the most able Chancellor of the Exchequer since the Second World War (Dell 1996: 491). His series of speeches as Financial Secretary was excellent and he was one of the architects of the Medium Term Financial Strategy. Given his expertise many people are puzzled about how Lawson lost control of inflation. Was it merely a technical expert being too close to things so that he lost perspective, in a way that a lay person would not have done? One of Lawson's flaws was that he was overconfident. A lesser man would have seen the pit in front of him in 1988 and would not have fallen into it – an analogy is the way a con man targets the most able person in sight because it never enters the able person's head that anyone could possibly con him.

Lawson also appears to have revelled in making deals on the world stage during the Plaza Agreement and the Louvre Accord, with full media attention, and being voted the most successful finance minister. ERM was a natural extension to these agreements. When sterling was shadowing the Deutschmark he gave instructions about the amount of intervention direct to Eddie George at the Bank, unusually bypassing both the Permanent Secretary of the Treasury and the Governor, although both were kept in touch with what was happening.[18] This is another example of him apparently enjoying making deals. Another part of his character was that, like many clever people, he wanted to pioneer new things and was restless; that is, he liked change and had a low boredom threshold. There is no doubt that by 1985 he had become incensed by Margaret Thatcher's refusal to follow his recommendation to join ERM and her attitude to him at the various seminars that followed. This appears to have become an obsession that subsequently clouded his judgement (Oliver 1997: 100 and 137–41).

Monetary Background

In spite of Howe having hit his published targets in the immediate preceding period, by the time Lawson became Chancellor the extraordinary behaviour of the published data in the early 1980s meant that broad money (sterling M3) – and by association monetarism – had become discredited as far as most people were concerned. This was serious for anyone wanting to use targets for managing expectations. As shown in more detail in Appendix 2, the published data for sterling M3 had been inflated by the unwinding of the 'bill' and 'euro' leaks associated with the corset. Further, banks had been allowed to start competing with building societies for mortgage business and had acquired a large share of this market, which inflated their deposits as well as their loans. As the two types of institution became similar, M4 – which includes the deposits of both types – became a better indicator of the underlying behaviour of broad money than sterling M3. All this meant that the targets for sterling M3 had first to be adjusted and then sterling M3 had to be replaced by M4. The result was serious damage to the credibility of the targets.

It is not surprising therefore that Lawson conducted a review of monetary policy in June 1983 when he became Chancellor. In March 1984 he decided to supplement the target for sterling M3 with one for M0. Monetarists who advocated MBC were not impressed by demand-side control of M0 and it also went down very badly with City opinion and financial journalists. The Bank initially treated the measure with open contempt (Lawson 1992: 454). M0 lacked 'street credibility', had no great effect on inflationary expectations and was more or less useless for political purposes. Monetary targets had lost credibility and Lawson wanted to replace them with an exchange rate target.

Lawson's Beliefs

Lawson has set out his economic beliefs more clearly than has either of his predecessors. Two key documents are his memoirs and his Mais Lecture in 1984. His memoirs describe how attempts in the 1970s to sustain output and activity in the face of rising prices had come to grief and that total spending in the economy should be limited to a rise sufficiently rapid to allow reasonable real growth in an environment of price stability. According to him the key decision at the end of the 1970s was to abandon attempts to 'set' real variables – for example real economic growth or full employment – and instead to define objectives in money terms (Lawson 1992: 416). He gave four ways of doing this. They were: (1) a nominal GDP objective, (2) a money supply target, (3) a price level objective,[19] and (4) an exchange rate objective. Lawson described the choice between these ways of defining monetary objectives as a 'second order' decision (Lawson 1992: 420). The crucial statement of his attitude to the choice between them comes on page 421 of his memoirs: 'It is perfectly sensible to target the money supply in some countries and at some times, and to target the exchange rate at others.'

In 1978–79 Lawson was arguing for an exchange rate target. He did this as a columnist in *Financial Weekly*, 'in support of the idea of Britain's full EMS membership' (Lawson 1992: 111).

In 1979 he argued for a monetary target: 'When I joined the Government in 1979, inflation was rising so fast that I felt the best *for the time being* was to concentrate on domestic monetary policy and leave sterling to market forces' (Lawson 1992: 111, emphasis added).

In 1981 he reverted to arguing for an exchange rate target. He sent a long note to Howe on 15 June, with inflation on the way down, arguing that 'we should take advantage of our forthcoming presidency [of the EC in the second half of 1981] to join the EMS' (Lawson 1992: 111). He sent another memo to Howe on 14 September 1981: '[We are] receiving increasing evidence of the weakness of sterling M3 as a reliable proxy for underlying monetary conditions, without any greater confidence being able to be attached to any of the other monetary aggregates. This clearly strengthens the case for moving over to an exchange rate discipline' (Lawson 1992: 112). Howe (1994: 274) confirms that Lawson was arguing 'cogently' for entry into ERM in the second half of 1981. The review of monetary policy that Lawson initiated on becoming Chancellor in 1983 led the Second Permanent Secretary at the Treasury (Geoffrey Littler) to recommend joining ERM (Lawson 1992: 451). Lawson states that he did not believe that 'the time was ripe' at the time to persuade the Prime Minister and that he had to wait until 1985 (Lawson 1992: 484–5). In January 1985 he judged that the time was ripe. He had his first serious internal meeting in the Treasury about joining ERM on 11 January. He had his first meeting with the Prime Minister on 28 January (Lawson 1992: 486–7).

In spite of the above, close associates of Lawson appear to have thought that he was serious about monetarism. Indeed, Lawson has described himself to be one of the

> practical monetarists ... who genuinely believe that it is essential to control monetary growth, but that this cannot be done precisely in a sophisticated and free economy, and that the task can be made less difficult by having regard to market credibility and expectations – which has a bearing on the target selected for publication at any particular time.[20]

Some of the confusion may be because Lawson defines a monetarist in a peculiar way, as the following quotations from *The View From No. 11* show:

- 'All of us who opted for the second alternative [controlling nominal rather than real GDP] were monetarists of sorts' (Lawson 1992: 421).
- 'It is obvious that an exchange rate objective is monetarism at one remove' (Lawson 1992: 419).
- 'The question is – or should be – a strictly practical one: which form of monetarism is the least difficult to operate successfully in practice?' (Lawson 1992: 419).

In short, Lawson includes anyone who advocates an exchange rate target, rather than a money supply target, or both at various times, in his definition of monetarist.[21] To put it mildly, Milton Friedman would not agree!

Returning to the choice between the intermediate targets, if their main purpose is political the choice between them is indeed not one of principle. When discussing their relative merits Lawson stresses the importance of presentation and public perception of policy. For example, a price level or an exchange rate objective is much more easily understood than a nominal GDP objective or a money supply target, the presumption being that they will have a greater effect on expectations. It may be noted that all these, apart from nominal GDP, have been tried since 1979.[22] A money supply target was used between the Conservatives coming to power in May 1979 and Lawson starting to shadow the Deutschmark in March 1987. An exchange rate objective was dominant between October 1990 and September 1992, when the UK was a member of ERM. An inflation rate objective has been used since the UK was forced to leave ERM in September 1992.

The overall conclusion is that Lawson was not a monetarist as defined either in this book or by Milton Friedman, and that he clearly gave priority to the politics of targets.

MARGARET THATCHER

Before she became Prime Minister, Margaret Thatcher claimed that she was a monetarist. She publicly announced her acceptance of monetarism in the 1968 Conservative Political Centre lecture and later acknowledged that Joseph's Preston speech was 'one of the most powerful and persuasive analyses I have ever read' which convinced her that 'we must turn the Party around towards Keith's way of thinking, preferably under Keith's leadership' (Thatcher 1995: 255 and 257). Thatcher's endorsement of Joseph's views can be seen in her approval of the drafting of *The Right Approach* which was presented to the Conservative Party Conference in October 1976. The document called for new targets for monetary growth (Conservative Central Office 1976). By late 1977, *The Right Approach to the Economy* had been drafted, which was intended to form the basis of the next election manifesto. *The Right Approach to the Economy* was more doctrinaire than *The Right Approach*, drawing its passages on the money supply almost verbatim from Joseph's Preston speech (Howe *et al.* 1977).

After she became Prime Minister, Margaret Thatcher could have joined her colleagues and become disillusioned with monetarism and changed her views, but there are three pieces of evidence which indicate that she did not.

The first piece of evidence can be found in *The Downing Street Years*. Whereas Margaret Thatcher has written about her general economic philosophy at length, there are only two passages in the book where she explicitly discusses her views on monetarism in the context of the 1980s. These are worth considering as they highlight the very clear differences between the beliefs of the Prime Minister and Lawson.

In the first passage, Thatcher writes about monetarism within the context of the MTFS at the beginning of the 1980s. She argues that the reduction in the rate of growth of the money stock was essential to reduce inflation permanently and that, at the start of that decade, the money supply was going to be controlled through adjustments in interest rates (Thatcher 1993: 97–9). In the second section, she reviews the implementation of monetarism in the 1980s. She concedes that during the early 1980s many of the monetary indicators were often 'distorted, confusing and volatile' and, because of this, the level of the exchange rate came to be monitored as a supplementary indicator of monetary conditions. She does however again assert that price stability can best be achieved by controlling the money supply rather than following an exchange rate objective (Thatcher 1993: 688–9).

The second piece of evidence is her strong and consistent opposition to the ERM. As mentioned earlier, Howe records her opposition at the formal meeting in 1979 after exchange controls were removed. At the next meeting in 1982, the one at which Howe, Carrington, Richardson, McMahon, Wass and Walters were present, she demolished the argument for joining the ERM, although she did allow the 'when the time is ripe' condition to continue. She subsequently opposed all Lawson's attempts to persuade her to join. She did not concede until 1990, when John Major was Chancellor. Her refusal was based on her understanding that control of the money supply was incompatible with having a target for the exchange rate. What comes across from the two extracts from *The Downing Street Years* is Margaret Thatcher's belief that the targets for the money supply were an intermediate target for controlling nominal GDP and that if the exchange rate became an objective of monetary policy, rather than an indicator, monetarism would have been abandoned. Thus, in contrast to Lawson, Margaret Thatcher did not view the choice between the money supply and the exchange rate as a 'second order' decision. In her own words, 'the only effective way to control inflation is by using interest rates to control the money supply [and if] you set interest rates in order to stick at a particular exchange rate you are steering by a different and potentially more wayward star' (Thatcher 1993: 690).

The third piece of evidence about the strength of her views is her refusal in October 1989, under pressure from Lawson and Howe, to dismiss Alan Walters as her personal economic adviser, which prompted the resignation of Lawson. While Walters and Lawson had appeared to share a similar economic philosophy in the early 1980s, by the end of the decade the situation had changed. Walters had clearly remained a genuine monetarist, and was vehemently opposed to joining the ERM with its 'half-baked' exchange rate arrangements (Walters 1988). In the wake of the episode when sterling was shadowing the Deutschmark, Margaret Thatcher came to rely more on the advice of Walters than that of her Chancellor. While Lawson was more committed to an exchange rate discipline, Walters was still a keen advocate of monetary control. Ironically, Lawson's resignation was followed swiftly by that of Walters and, in the event, Margaret Thatcher was left even more isolated with her monetarist beliefs. She was a genuine monetarist, who had become a lonely one.

Thus, despite being surrounded by politicians, advisers and officials who had been anti-monetarist, or who had advocated monetary targets merely to manage expectations, Margaret Thatcher had persisted alone in the Cabinet with her monetarist views. While she was aware that Lawson's position had changed, it is not clear the extent to which she realized how Middleton and some other senior officials in the Treasury and the Bank were merely managers of expectations. It appears that they may have been less than frank with their advice to her.[23]

POSTSCRIPT: A PERSONAL NOTE BY PEPPER

Lawson has described how I had 'established a private line to Margaret Thatcher when she was Leader of the Opposition' (Lawson 1992: 80). In the second half of the 1970s I had sessions with her before each budget and party conference, and spasmodic meetings at other times. (After she became Prime Minister the meetings gradually waned. I like to think that this was mainly for two reasons. First, the official machine inevitably takes over the role of briefing the Prime Minister on current financial events. Secondly, I was a stockbroker specializing in the gilt-edged market and any discussion of whether interest rates were at the right level or monetary policy was too loose or too tight would have given me insider-trading information. A Prime Minister cannot talk to the likes of me in the same way as could the Leader of the Opposition. Mrs Thatcher did however remain on the circulation list for the Greenwell *Monetary Bulletins*, which started to argue that policy was much too tight in May 1980 (Pepper 1998: 147, 198) and dangerously loose in August 1987 (Pepper 1998: 151).)

As a monetary economist I saw two sides of Mrs Thatcher's character. The first was the combination of research scientist and barrister. As a research scientist she had a passion for knowledge. As a barrister she was used to mastering all the detail of a brief. She had a razor-sharp mind and would ruthlessly expose any sloppiness in analysis. Because of her insistence on mastering detail she became renowned for being the best-briefed person at meetings.

The other side of Mrs Thatcher was her strong convictions. These came in good part from her upbringing, which she has described in Chapter 1 of *The Path To Power*:

- She was born into a home 'which was practical, serious and intensely religious' (Thatcher 1995: 5).
- 'Life for poor people before the Second World War was very difficult; and it was not much easier for those who had worked hard, accumulating a nest egg, and achieved a precarious respectability. They lived on a knife-edge and feared that if some accident hit them, or if they relaxed their standards of thrift and diligence, they might be plunged into debt and poverty' (Thatcher 1995: 6). (This remark appears to be a personal one as her family were not well off, which is illustrated by her walking home from school for lunch, walking four miles a day back and forth, because it was more economical than school lunch (Thatcher 1995: 17).)
- 'These upright qualities, which entailed a refusal to alter your convictions just because others disagreed with you or because you became unpopular, were instilled into me from my earliest days' (Thatcher 1995: 7).
- 'Nothing in our house was wasted, and we always lived within our means. The worst you could say about another family was that they "lived up to the hilt"' (Thatcher 1995: 121).

Keith Joseph was the other strong influence on her. She was a true disciple of his. The dedication of *The Path To Power* to Joseph is an illustration of the extent to which she regarded him as a very special person. From him she accepted the general proposition that excessive monetary growth leads in due course to a rise in inflation.

Summarizing, Mrs Thatcher hated inflation. It was a country living beyond its means. The consequence was that the real value of people's hard-earned savings was eroded, which she thought immoral. Because she hated inflation, she attached great importance to preventing excessive monetary growth. *She was a monetarist more by conviction than scientific argument.*

The two sides of Mrs Thatcher's character sometimes came into conflict. When someone is describing their convictions it is often difficult for anyone else to contribute to the conversation. Analysis and detail have to wait until later. The result was that the detailed arguments could go by default because time was up as Mrs Thatcher had another appointment.

It must be remembered that no politician likes raising interest rates and, if rates do have to be raised, they choose the timing to minimize odium. Mrs Thatcher's vision of a property-owning democracy and the effect of high rates on the housing market meant that she was no exception. Her reluctance to raise interest rates was well known and this gave many people the impression that she gave higher priority to keeping rates down over controlling the money supply. She was however well aware that lower inflation was the key to reducing interest rates and that interest rates could not be held down for long if inflation were not controlled. The clash between control of the money supply and low interest rates only occurs in the short run; there is no clash over the long term. Mrs Thatcher accepted that control of the money supply was essential if interest rates were to be permanently reduced. Nevertheless, the argument had to be stated correctly if she was to be persuaded to raise interest rates. This brings us to the various people who were in contact with her about monetary policy.

Mrs Thatcher's Advisers on Monetary Policy

Pepper, 1974–79 (unofficial, to the Leader of the Opposition), 1979–83 (spasmodic)

I was learning from experience throughout the period. As I learnt, my analysis became tighter. With the benefit of hindsight my mind is now much clearer than it was at the time. (I suspect that this applies to most of the 'actors', including Lawson.) In the 1970s my thinking was clear about distortions to broad money (for example, about 'round tripping' and the 'bill leak') but I only clarified my views on narrow money, as an indicator, versus broad money early in 1980.

Treasury/Howe, 1979–83

When Howe was Chancellor and the Treasury team went round to Number 10 Downing Street to discuss monetary policy, there was a genuine discussion involving all of the participants. This was Howe's style, but note the qualifications of the participants:

- Howe – according to Dell, he did not possess the technical qualifications to choose between the different measures of money (Dell 1996: 454).

- Wass – according to a Treasury ex-minister, he was one of 'the cynical monetarist who believe it is all a lot of mumbo-jumbo designed to impress the markets who for some strange reason think it mattered'.[24]
- Middleton – he was a political monetarist as defined in this book.
- Burns – while at the London Business School he was an international monetarist who believed that the transmission mechanism was via the effect of a monetary squeeze on the exchange rate and the subsequent effect of the exchange rate on domestic inflation.

It is doubtful if Mrs Thatcher was briefed on the difference between genuine monetarism and political monetarism as defined in this book.

Walters, 1981–mid 1984 (full time), mid 1984–May 1989 (part time), May 1989–October 1989 (full time)

Walters was a genuine monetarist. He was *not* one of the people who cannot see the wood for the trees. His overall assessments of situations were excellent but, in spite of being an expert, he was sometimes cavalier with detail. (This combination may have been one of the reasons why he appealed to Mrs Thatcher; the mixture of intuition and analysis was in some ways similar.)

Niehans, February 1981

Mrs Thatcher discussed the Niehans (1981) report with Walters in depth in February 1981. She was fully exposed at that time to the detail of narrow money versus broad money.

Treasury/Lawson, 1983–89

Lawson had a different style from Howe. The main discussions occurred within the Treasury. Lawson describes, for example, how 'I gradually brought my officials round to my way of thinking on the ERM' (Lawson 1992: 486). During meetings with the Prime Minister only the agreed position was articulated, with individual participants not putting forward their personal views. Although she might have felt it frustrating, it would have been improper for the Prime Minister to ask an official if he agreed personally with the position being advanced by the Chancellor.

Bank of England 1979–89

When the Governor of the Bank went round to Number 10, with the Chancellor, to argue for a rise in interest rates, the main argument deployed by the Governor was that there would be a collapse in confidence in either the foreign exchange or the discount market, or both, if the Prime Minister did not agree to a rise. The argument was expressed in this way because the Bank considered that it was up to the Treasury to advance the economic arguments and that its particular expertise was its first-hand knowledge of markets. Mrs Thatcher had little confidence in the Bank's reading of market psychology and her reaction to the case advanced by the Bank was usually very hostile.

Figure 5.1 summarizes who was giving advice on monetary policy to Mrs Thatcher at different times. Walters went back to the US in May 1984. Lawson, having whipped the Treasury officials into line, was advocating ERM from the beginning of 1985. The Bank was only arguing market psychology. By the second half of the 1980s Mrs Thatcher had become isolated.

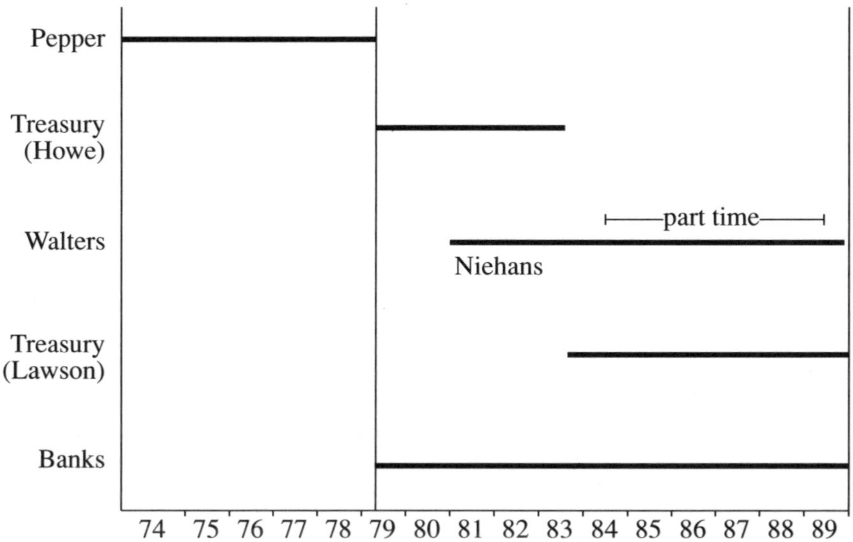

Figure 5.1 Monetary policy advisers to Margaret Thatcher, 1974–89

Summary

Inflation is evil. There is a powerful moral case for embracing monetarism. Mrs Thatcher was a monetarist by moralist conviction.

6. Summary and conclusions of Part I

A consistent theme has been building up. It started with things not quite what they seem to be. The underwriting of the Treasury bill issue, the reserve asset ratio and the power to call for special deposits under Competition and Credit Control were merely devices to reinforce the Bank's control over interest rates. The outright deception under the corset came next. After he left office Healey declared himself to be a disbelieving monetarist, who embraced monetary targets merely for political purposes. The officials Fforde and Middleton have, in effect, also declared themselves to be political monetarists.

The authors attach considerable importance to Middleton's statement, 'the main effort must be directed towards maintaining the credibility and reputation of macro economic policy so that financial markets behave in a way which generally supports it'. It was not an off-the-cuff remark but the main conclusion of a formal lecture by the most senior civil servant in the Treasury. To obtain confirmation, a draft of the comments on the lecture was sent to Middleton and a meeting between him and Pepper followed. Middleton's first reaction was that the comments were 'about right', although he did go on to say that he had tried to move away from Keynesian economics towards monetarism. He confirmed that he had been deliberately misleading when giving the briefing about the introduction to the Green Paper *Monetary Control*. There is, however, a possibility that Middleton was still being misleading; his NIESR Jubilee Lecture may have been an attempt to rewrite history in his favour. Pepper's conclusion was that the lecture should be taken at face value for two reasons. First, the benefit to Middleton of such a rewrite of history is not clear; his motive for misinformation appears to be much less powerful than on the first occasion. Secondly, as Pepper was leaving the room at the end of the meeting Middleton expressed concern that Pepper might have thought he had behaved dishonourably when giving the briefing about the introduction to *Monetary Control*.[25] The concern appeared to Pepper to be genuine. If it was not, Middleton had gone to extraordinary lengths to confuse.

Middleton had not behaved in a dishonourable way. To understand this, the nature of the British civil service has to be appreciated. Unlike the US, UK civil servants do not change when a government alters. Suppose the change is from Labour to Conservative. Officials who were implementing their Labour political masters' policies before the election have the task of implementing those of their Conservative political masters after the election. They argue the case accordingly. Overnight black can become white and white can become black. An outsider who meets this for the first time can be amazed by the transformation. It is indeed one of the skills of senior civil servants; it is part of their professionalism. Civil servants have no real choice in that they have either to support their minister or resign (Lawson 1992: 486). If they disagree with the reasons for a policy that are advanced by their political masters they may have their own ones for believing that the policy is desirable. This can become close to them having a hidden agenda.

Further, any official who has regular contact with people in a financial market must be able to tell falsehoods fluently or else he or she will divulge insider-trading information. Professionals in a financial market are past masters at ferreting out information. If they know an official well they can ask a question and get something confirmed if the official refuses to answer, pauses before giving the answer or even from the intonation of his or her voice. Put bluntly, a fact of life, whether people like to admit it or not, is that an official sometimes has no alternative but to tell a lie, especially to a guru of the gilt-edged market, who should be well aware that this may be so (something similar can apply for press officers who get too close to the media).[26]

Overall, the saga disclosed in Part I is one of official attempts to manage expectations, misinformation, manipulation and deception.[27] This started before the Thatcher years and has carried on since then with the 'spinning' under New Labour. Our conclusions are as follows:

- First, that economic historians who are brave enough to study contemporary history must be especially cynical about what politicians and officials say when they are attempting to influence markets.
- The second conclusion is about Howe's Chancellorship. Howe's strength was that he was determined that the UK should adopt voluntarily the sort of policy that the IMF had imposed in 1976. He did not, however, possess the technical qualifications to choose between the different measures of money and the different forms of control offered to him. Dell has argued that Howe's monetarism looked like Treasury policy. Middleton has stated that this policy was political monetarism.
- Thirdly, Lawson was much too competent technically to be enveloped by the Treasury. He thought of an exchange rate target as a form of monetarism. He was not therefore a monetarist as defined either in this book or by Milton Friedman. He also gave priority to the *politics* of targets.
- The fourth conclusion is the extent to which Margaret Thatcher became isolated. Mrs Thatcher was a monetarist more by conviction than by scientific argument and although she was a genuine monetarist she was

surrounded by political monetarists, if they were monetarists at all. When officials were misleading financial markets it is possible that they may also have misled the Prime Minister. They may have been less than frank with their advice.

The overall conclusion of Part I is that, in spite of the instinct of the Prime Minister, the authorities never attempted to control the supply *of money, by controlling the reserve base of the banking system, as the North American and Swiss schools of monetarism argued they should, and that they only paid lip service to controlling the* demand *for money, although they did attempt some control over the counterparts of broad money. The experiment in the 1980s was mainly an exercise in political monetarism.*

PART II

Policy Dilemmas

7. A type of supply-side control: control via the 'counterparts'

North American readers are urged to read Appendix 3, which describes the difference between the US and UK monetary systems, before reading this chapter.

Money can be created in two ways. Governments can 'print money' and bankers can create 'fountain-pen money'.

PRINTING-PRESS MONEY

Over the years governments have financed themselves by 'printing money' in various ways. In olden days, when coins were the most important form of money, kings debased the coinage to finance wars. After paper money became more important governments resorted to the printing press, for example during the Weimar Republic in Germany in the 1920s. In today's environment bank deposits are a more important form of money than notes and the modern way of printing money is for a government to borrow from the banking system.

(In more detail, suppose that the government pays for some expenditure by sending someone a cheque. When the person cashes the cheque, his or her bank deposit will rise, as will the bank's deposit with the Bank of England (the government banks with the Bank). The bank's additional deposit will be surplus to its requirements and the bank will invest the money in Treasury bills.[28] The Bank will sell these as part of its daily money market operations to finance the government's deficit. The result of these routine transactions is that the money supply will have risen, as the person's bank deposit has risen, and the government will have borrowed from the banking system, as the bank's holdings of Treasury bills have risen.)

The Exchequer's main need for finance is to cover the public sector net cash requirement, but it also needs funds to finance any increase in the UK's foreign exchange reserves less any money raised directly from foreigners, for example through foreign purchases of gilt-edged stock. The Exchequer's main source of finance is borrowing from the non-bank private sector, with sales of gilt-edged stock again being the main example. Any finance not met from this source is in the short run borrowed more or less automatically from the banking sector. The position is summarized in the following three 'accounting identities':

Accounting Identity 1
The public sector's net cash requirement
plus
the increase in the UK's gold and foreign exchange reserves less public sector borrowing from abroad
less
sales of public sector debt to the non-bank private sector
equals
the public sector's residual need for finance.

Accounting Identity 2
The public sector's residual need for finance
equals
government borrowing from the banking system.

Accounting Identity 3
Government borrowing from the banking system
equals
the supply of printing-press money.

The public sector net cash requirement is heavily influenced by fiscal policy. Changes in the UK's gold and foreign exchange reserves depend on the policy regarding intervention in the foreign exchange market. Sales of public sector debt are a matter for funding and sterilization policies (funding policy is how the government's domestic deficit is financed, whereas sterilization policy is how foreign exchange intervention is financed). The combination of these four policies – namely, fiscal, funding, foreign exchange intervention and sterilization policies – determines the supply of printing-press money. It follows that the supply of printing-press money can in theory be controlled by a combination of these four policies. In practice the weapon used to fine tune the total is sales of public sector debt to the non-bank private sector.

FOUNTAIN-PEN MONEY

Fountain-pen money is created by banks when they make a loan. The simplest case is when two people use the same bank and one of them increases his overdraft when he makes a payment to the other. The latter's bank deposit rises.

In the bank's books, loans rise on the asset side of the balance sheet and deposits rise on the liability side. The money supply increases as the entry is made in the bank's books. Until the late twentieth century the records were kept manually by clerks using fountain pens and the money was created at the stroke of a banker's pen. This is the explanation of the term 'fountain-pen money'. In more detail, the accounting identity for fountain-pen money is:

Accounting Identity 4
Banks' sterling lending to the private sector
less
banks' borrowing in foreign currency and from abroad
less
the growth of banks' non-deposit liabilities
equals
the supply of fountain-pen money.

Under the UK's system of monetary control the supply of fountain-pen money cannot be controlled directly. The method of control employed has been to vary short-term interest rates to influence the demand for loans. It has been totally inadequate.

THE 'COUNTERPARTS' OF BROAD MONEY

Broad money consists of printing-press money plus fountain-pen money. This leads to the next Accounting Identity:

Accounting Identity 5
The supply of printing-press money
plus
the supply of fountain-pen money
equals
the growth of M3.

The final Accounting Identity is a summary:

Accounting Identity 6
Public sector net cash requirement
less
sales of public sector debt to the non-bank private sector
less
public sector borrowing in foreign currency or from abroad
plus

banks' sterling lending to the private sector
less
banks' borrowing in foreign currency and from abroad
less
growth of banks' non-deposit liabilities
equals
growth of M3.

The elements in Accounting Identity 6 are known as the 'counterparts' of M3. A similar identity, replacing banks with banks and building societies, can be constructed for M4. The data for the calendar years 1985 to 1989 are shown in Table 7.1.

Table 7.1 The counterparts of M4

£ million	1985	1986	1987	1988	1989
Public sector net cash requirement	7445	2316	–1424	–12132	–9282
Purchases (–) of M4 public sector net debt by M4 private sector	–8085	–5850	–4229	3812	12736
External and foreign currency finance of public sector (–)	–3142	–2056	7157	3463	–3384
M4 lending	34028	47076	54031	82322	88927
External and foreign currency transactions of Monetary Financial Institutions	519	–602	–5212	–11957	–13657
Net non-deposit liabilities of banks and building societies (–)	–4891	–6004	–6580	–12994	–10585
Growth of M4	25874	34855	43746	52514	64755

Source: Bank of England (1998: Table 6.1).

It should be noted that funding policy can be used not only to control the supply of printing-press money but also to offset any fluctuations in fountain-pen money. In the contribution to the discussion following Pepper (1990b), Congdon called funding policy a supply-side measure. In particular, excessive growth of bank lending can be offset by 'overfunding'.

RELATIONSHIP BETWEEN THE COUNTERPARTS

The relationship between broad money and its counterparts is complex. Taking the PSNCR as an example, if tax rates are altered both the PSNCR and broad money will tend to be affected in the same direction; both will tend to rise if taxation is reduced and fall if taxation is increased. On the other hand, if discretionary fiscal policy remains unchanged the PSNCR will tend to rise in a recession and fall in a boom, because of variations in tax revenue and unemployment benefits, and so on. Bank lending to the private sector will, however, tend to do the opposite, rising in a boom and falling in a recession. The fluctuations in bank lending tend to be greater than those in the PSNCR and, because of this, broad money may fall when the PSNCR increases and rise when the PSNCR decreases. In short, the relationship between the two is not a simple correlation, but changes in *discretionary* fiscal policy do affect the growth of broad money.

8. Overfunding: a useful tool or a cosmetic device?

HISTORICAL BACKGROUND

The 1939–45 war was largely financed by the government borrowing from the banking system. By the end of the war banks' holdings of government debt were huge and bank lending to the private sector was relatively small. During the next twenty-five years banks' holdings of government debt were progressively run down as private sector lending increased. Banks' holdings of central government debt as a percentage of their total sterling liabilities fell from about 75 per cent in 1953 to about 30 per cent in 1970. Following the removal of the controls on bank lending to the private sector, when Competition and Credit Control was introduced in 1971, private sector lending exploded. It was the main cause of excessive monetary growth during the Barber boom, as described in Chapter 1.

After monetary targets were introduced in 1976, private sector lending continued to be buoyant. In an attempt to hit the published targets a policy of overfunding was followed; that is, more gilt-edged stocks were sold than was needed to finance the PSNCR. Printing-press money previously created was destroyed to offset excessive growth of fountain-pen money. The government repaid the banks, which led to a further decline in banks' holdings of government debt.

THE BANK'S BILL MOUNTAIN

As Figure 8.1 shows, by 1981 banks' holdings of government debt had fallen to a level that was a working minimum. The total of Treasury bills in issue had fallen from about £7,000m in 1976 to just over £1,000m in 1981. With no Treasury bills remaining to purchase, the Bank started to purchase commercial bills. Its holdings rose from virtually zero in July 1981 to over £7,500m by March 1982 (Figure 8.2). By 1984 it had risen to over £10,000m. By mid 1985 the Bank's bill mountain had reached £14,000m (source of data: various Greenwell *Monetary Bulletins*).

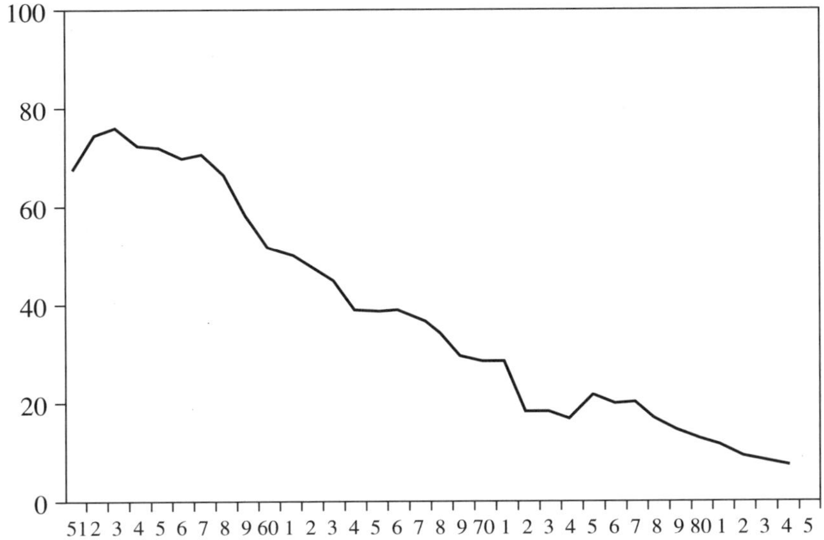

Figure 8.1 Banks' holdings of government debt, 1951–84 (as % of banks' sterling deposits)

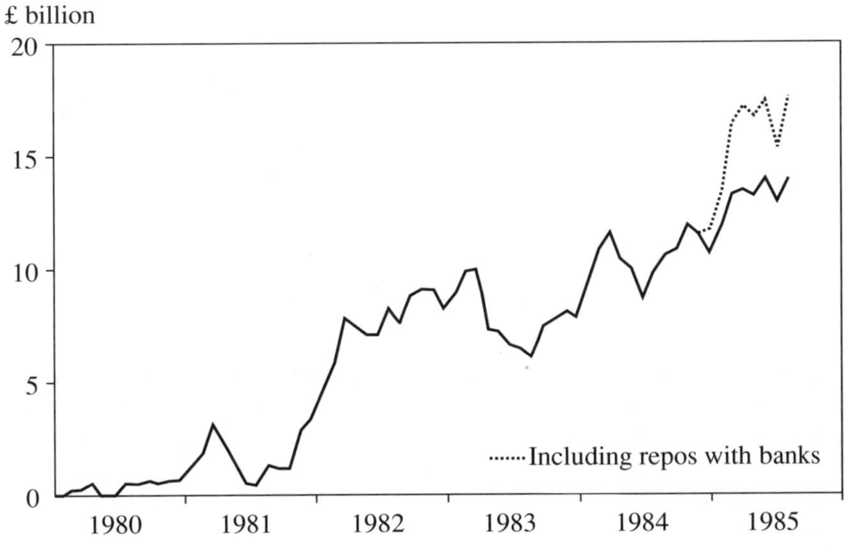

Figure 8.2 Bank of England bill mountain, 1980–85

Many people considered the effect of overfunding on the money supply to be cosmetic. Lawson agreed: 'overfunding was essentially a way of massaging the money numbers to make it look as if monetary policy was tighter than it was' (see Lawson 1992: 449, 458).[29] The mistake that he and the others made was to concentrate on the effect of overfunding on credit and not on the fountain-pen money created by the credit. Whereas it was correct to argue that the effect on credit was cosmetic, because the Bank was itself providing the finance previously provided by banks, the effect on the money supply was not cosmetic. Lawson made the mistake committed by most non-monetary economists who focus on the economic decision associated with a credit transaction and ignore the impact of any additional fountain-pen money that has been created. *The credit effect is a one-off. The monetary effect continues.* Suppose, for example, that someone finances a new factory by borrowing from a bank. The credit transaction is associated with the increase in industrial investment and hence in GDP. The direct impact on GDP is a one-off. The increase in fountain-pen money created by the bank loan has a subsequent continuing effect, as successive holders of the bank deposits spend them.

Borrowing from a bank, issuing a corporate bond or issuing a commercial bill that is sold to the Bank are all ways in which a borrower can obtain credit. The trouble with a bank acting as the financial intermediary occurs because the funds for the credit come from an increase in fountain-pen money. If a corporate bond is issued, the money for the credit comes from long-term savers. If a commercial bill is issued and sold to the Bank, the money comes from the issue of gilt-edged stock by the Bank; that is, again from long-term savers. The difference is merely that the Bank rather than the borrower has issued the bond.

In the event Lawson abandoned overfunding and suspended the target for broad money (sterling M3) in October 1985. Monetary growth promptly accelerated. As explained in the next chapter, asset-price inflation then gathered momentum and product-price inflation followed, albeit with a longer time lag than usual.

PROBLEMS WITH OVERFUNDING

Although overfunding is not cosmetic it must be admitted that there were, and are, problems with it. A basic one, mentioned by Lawson, is that sales of long-dated gilt-edged stock and purchases of commercial bills by the Bank raise long-term rates of interest relative to short-term rates. This encourages companies to borrow from a bank rather than raise money by issuing bonds. A *persistent* policy of overfunding leads in the long run to even greater reliance on bank lending. The policy eventually becomes unsustainable but this does not mean that overfunding is not a useful short-run weapon.

Another difficulty in the mid 1980s, which Lawson did not mention, was irritating rather than basic. The Bank's huge holdings of bills had to be rolled over as they matured. The rollovers (the issue of new bills to replace the maturing ones) became so large that the transactions dominated the bill market and the Bank was perceived to set rates throughout the maturity spectrum. The media then interpreted a change in any rate as an official signal about interest rates. As a result, the Bank grew reluctant to change a rate in case the change was misinterpreted. An acute difficulty arose when there was a change in market expectations about the future course of interest rates. If free market forces had been allowed to prevail, the term structure of rates would have altered to reflect the new expectations. In the event the Bank did not change its rates, ran into a huge volume of arbitrage transactions and made substantial losses if market expectations turned out to be correct. The solution should have been to allow the term structure of interest rates to reflect expectations. In general, the Bank can control a single rate of interest in the money market without running into massive speculation but not two or more rates with different terms. Signals about interest rates should have been confined to a single rate and the media should have been educated accordingly.

Another problem was arbitrage transactions. The Bank's huge purchases of commercial bills pushed up their prices and reduced the rate of discount on bills. Companies were able to raise finance by issuing bills and using the funds to purchase certificates of deposit issued by banks (CDs) for a risk-free profit. This inflated the data for the broad money supply, distorting them upwards.

Summarizing, the problems were quite severe but they were definitely minor in comparison with the harm to the UK economy during the inflationary boom that followed the suspension of overfunding in 1985.

9. Asset-price inflation

This book does not discuss the rational expectations theory of asset prices in detail. What follows does not argue that the theory is incorrect but merely advances the liquidity theory of asset prices as a complementary theory. The combination of the two theories explains far more than the rational expectations theory alone.

Economists use the phrase 'the demand for broad money' to denote persons' and companies' desire to hold money balances. Their demand to hold money balances depends on their income and wealth, and the attractiveness of money relative to other assets. The supply of money is a distinct concept and refers to the level of money balances (that is, notes, coin and bank deposits) actually in being. In general, the demand for money is not equal to the supply of money. The system is rarely in equilibrium, as explained in Appendix 4.

If the supply of money is in excess of the current demand for money, at the current level of economic activity and asset prices, some of the excess will be spent on goods and services and economic activity will rise as a consequence. The result in due course, and after a long and variable time lag, will be inflation higher than would otherwise have been the case. This type of inflation may be called product-price inflation.

If the supply of money exceeds the current demand for money, part of the excess will be spent on assets. This is particularly likely to be the case if fountain-pen money is being created as a result of people borrowing to acquire assets, because the money so created is also likely to be used to acquire further assets. The result will be a rise in asset prices. This may be called asset-price inflation.

In the mid 1980s Lawson thought that the stock market was rising in recognition of his abilities and that it was a vote of confidence in him. He did not understand that excessive growth of the money supply was leading to asset-price inflation. Pepper became aware of this failure as a result of his membership of Lawson's Group of Outside Independent Economists (the Gooies) (Lawson 1992: 80–81; Pepper 1998: 25–6).

An example will make asset-price inflation clearer. Suppose that there has been a recession, coupled with a fall in the stock market. As the recession comes to an end, the stock market recovers. In these circumstances a company is quite likely to make a bid for another company and to finance the takeover by borrowing from a bank. The stock market will rise when the bid is announced. When the bid goes through, holders of shares in the company will receive bank deposits in exchange for their shares. They may well subsequently reinvest the proceeds in other shares. It is important to realize that such a reinvestment does not destroy the bank deposit, because the seller of the shares in which the reinvestment is being made will receive the deposit in exchange for the shares. For example, if someone switches out of a bank deposit into BP, say, the seller of BP will receive the deposit. If this person reinvests the money in Marks & Spencer, say, the person who sells Marks & Spencer will receive the deposit. This third person may reinvest the money, and so on. Each time the reinvestment takes place the market will tend to rise. Again, the initial credit transaction has a one-off effect whereas the consequential increase in the money supply has a continuing effect. If excessive growth of credit persists, the continuing monetary effects compound. The result can easily be the formation of a bubble in asset prices.

FINANCIAL BUBBLES

In more detail, markets respond if people persistently have money that they wish to invest. Prices rise as they buy shares. Explanations are then invented to account for the rise. At its simplest there are always bullish and bearish factors present in a market. If the market rises the bullish ones are advanced as the explanation. The truth is that these factors have already been discounted and the explanations for the behaviour of the market are invalid. The erroneous explanations nevertheless receive publicity and affect sentiment. People tend to be bullish when prices are rising and, conversely, bearish when they are falling. Few, if any, observers of a market dispute that sentiment *can* be influenced by the direction in which the market is moving.[30] A rising market can encourage more purchases, which adds further to the rise. This does not always happen but it most certainly can happen.

There is a further point. Many speculators are influenced by intuition and this is often a reflection of the amount of money about. If people have money to invest not all the funds will be invested as they accrue; some will be allowed to accumulate. When unexpected good news occurs decision-taking inertia is broken. Accumulated funds are invested. The greater the accumulation of liquidity, the larger will be the rise in the market. The market's response to good news will be clear. In the opposite case, people needing to raise cash are often prompted into action by unexpected bad news. The size of the fall in the market depends on how many people are waiting to raise cash. If many people are waiting the market's response to bad news will be clear. Professionals who are close to a market observe how the market is reacting to news. A market tending to react to good news and to ignore bad gives the impression of wanting to go up; a market reacting to bad news and ignoring good gives the impression of wanting to go down. Speculators who rely on intuition are strongly influenced by the amount of money about, although they may not realize it. One result is that they often act as a crowd and crowd psychology becomes important. Further, the behaviour of crowds produces patterns in charts of the level of a market. This is the underlying explanation of chartism (more formally known as technical analysis), which has a further influence on speculators (Plummer 1989). Financial bubbles form as speculators operate as a crowd. Such bubbles developed progressively in both the UK and the US in 1986 and during the first three-quarters of 1987. For a full discussion of financial bubbles, especially the non-monetary factors, see Chancellor (1999), Kindleberger (1989) and Pepper (1994: Ch. 13).

Reverting to more conventional economics, it should be noted that the real rate of interest for financial transactions can diverge sharply from that for transactions in goods and services. The real rate is the nominal rate less expectations of inflation. Real rates diverge if expectations of asset-price inflation differ from expectations of product-price inflation. This will be the case when financial markets are rising at a time when product-price inflation is muted. If nominal interest rates are set at a level appropriate for expenditure on goods and services, very low or negative real rates for financial transactions will encourage further acquisition of assets.

THE EFFICIENT-MARKET HYPOTHESIS

Academics who believe in a simplistic version of the efficient-market hypothesis, and people who are influenced by them, do not accept the above analysis about financial bubbles. First it should be appreciated that the efficient-market hypothesis does not state that the level of the stock market correctly reflects the underlying fundamentals of corporate profitability, and so on. It merely states that people cannot consistently make money using existing available information; that is, prices merely reflect this information. Believers in a simplistic version of the hypothesis nevertheless argue that there are sufficient potential speculators to make sure that a market does reflect fundamentals. They argue that speculators will sell stocks if a market becomes fundamentally overvalued; that this will push prices back to the level justified by the fundamentals; and that this mechanism will prevent financial bubbles from occurring.

The answer to this argument is that people who understand financial bubbles and who are confident that a market is much higher than can be justified by fundamentals do not know when the bubble will burst. The danger is that shares will be sold too soon, that the market will carry on rising for some time, and that the rise will be substantial. Indeed the final rise in a market just before a bubble burst is frequently hectic. Departing from the herd can be very risky. An investment manager can lose his or her job. A fund management firm can lose clients. The firm may not even survive as an independent entity. The short-run risks can easily become unacceptably high.

In more detail, when people invest in stocks and shares they choose the shares that will maximize their expected yield, subject to minimizing risk. There is a trade-off between maximizing yield and minimizing risk. A basic mistake made by believers in a simplistic version of the efficient-market hypothesis is to confuse risk of loss with volatility and to focus on the latter. Investors are in fact more concerned by risk of loss ('downside uncertainty' in some academics' terminology) than by the volatility of a share's price. The distinction is especially important because risk of loss depends on the circumstances of an investor in contrast to the volatility of a share's price, which is the same irrespective of who the investor may be. A long-dated gilt-edged stock, for example, is a much riskier investment for a bank that has short-term liabilities than for a life office that is writing long-term without-profit business, but the volatility of the prices of long-dated gilt-edged stock is the same for both institutions. Risk of loss also depends on the liquidity of both an investor and the market as a whole. *Investors may confidently expect a transaction to result in abnormally high profits in the long term but risk of loss in the short term can rise to such an extent that the opportunity has to be declined.*

A more accurate version of the efficient-market hypothesis is that people cannot consistently make money using existing available information *without taking unacceptably high risk of loss, bearing in mind that risk of loss varies with the circumstances of an investor and the behaviour of a market.*

Practical experience indicates that believers in the simplistic version of the efficient-market hypothesis are wrong when they assert that financial bubbles cannot occur. They definitely do occur in practice. In short, belief in a simplistic version of the hypothesis inoculates too many economists from understanding the behaviour of financial markets. Lawson appears to have been influenced by them.

APPENDIX 9.1: TYPES OF TRADERS IN SECURITIES

A deduction from the efficient-market hypothesis is that the prices of securities only change when unexpected new information becomes available. This is usually interpreted to mean news about fundamentals, for example about the factors affecting corporate profitability. There is a second type of news. The appearance of unexpected persistent liquidity trades is important news for all investors.

'Liquidity Trades' and 'Portfolio Trades'

There are two basic reasons why someone purchases or sells a security. The first type of transaction occurs when someone needs either to raise cash or has surplus money to invest. This type of transaction may be called a 'liquidity trade'. The second type of transaction occurs when someone switches from one share into another, or into or out of cash, in the hope that the transaction will improve the return on a portfolio. A transaction of this second type may be called a 'portfolio trade'.

It may be noted that portfolio traders respond to very small changes in the expected return of one investment relative to another; they exploit small deviations in price. In contrast, quite large changes in returns do not have a quick effect on the aggregate level of savings in the economy, which influences the amount of money that people have available to invest, or on capital formation, which influences the need for funds by industry. Further, a government does not alter taxes or public expenditure, which influence its need for funds, merely because interest rates have changed a little. In short, liquidity trades are not as sensitive to changes in the expected return on investments or in the prices of securities as portfolio trades.

'Information Trades' and 'Price Trades'

Another distinction is between two types of portfolio trade. A trade can occur either because there has been some unexpected new information that affects the value of a share or because the price of a share has altered in spite of there not being any new information justifying the alteration. The first type of portfolio trade may be called an 'information trade'. The second may be called a 'price trade'.

'Efficient Prices'

When new information becomes available information traders act very quickly if they think that they can make a profit, with prices responding until no one else can do so. Prices then become 'efficient' once again.

Information trades establish efficient prices but liquidity trades move prices away from the efficient level. A sale of a share to raise money will initially depress the share's price. If the price falls without there being any news justifying the fall, price traders will normally judge the share to be cheap and will purchase it until the price reverts to the efficient level. In the opposite case of a liquidity purchase, the price of the share will initially rise. If there is no news justifying the rise, price traders will normally judge the share to be dear and will sell until the prices revert to the efficient level.

Summarizing, liquidity trades move prices away from the efficient level and price trades normally push prices back again. As the potential number of price trades is very large compared with liquidity trades, they are usually sufficiently numerous to be able to correct price discrepancies caused by liquidity trades.

Types of Information Trader

There are four types of information trader:

1. Intuitive traders, who detect how a market is reacting to news.
2. Technical analysts (chartists), who pay attention to patterns in charts.
3. Monetary analysts, who understand asset-price inflation (for example, clients of Lombard Street Research, London, and subscribers to the *Bank Credit Analyst*, Montreal).
4. Fundamental, who analysts try to forecast the trading conditions affecting companies and a company's profits, earnings per share, dividends and so on.

When the supply of money exceeds the demand for money, people tend to have money to invest and liquidity trades tend to be purchases. Prices of securities tend to rise as a result. Monetary analysts, intuitive traders and technical analysts follow the price rise and also purchase securities. Fundamental analysts sell, because prices have risen without there being unexpected news of fundamentals justifying the rise. There is a battle between the two groups. The former wins. The latter makes losses (at least on paper). Fundamental analysts start to lose confidence and the market rises further. As prices rise even further above the level justified by fundamentals, more selling on fundamental grounds may occur but these transactions also lose money. Fundamental selling then dries up as the risk of further losses if securities are sold becomes unacceptable.

10. Debt deflation

The effect of a financial bubble in the equity market is not merely financial. Wealth increases as a result of the rise in asset prices. Economic activity responds as people spend some of their increased wealth and as confidence improves. Part of the rise in the market is validated. The effect spirals upward. Financial bubbles do not, however, last forever. They eventually burst; asset prices fall and a downward spiral starts.

The downward spiral starts symmetrically with the previous upward spiral. The earlier rise in asset prices, confidence, wealth and expenditure on goods and services is balanced by falls in the downswing. But there is a danger of asymmetry because of the gearing, and associated concentration of risk, inherent in the banking system's balance sheet.

The process becomes asymmetrical during the downswing when the value of asset prices falls to a level at which the value of collateral in general is no longer sufficient to cover the bank loans being secured. There are various stages to this process. In order of intensity they are:

1. Borrowers become forced sellers of assets.
2. People start to go bankrupt.
3. Others retrench as they observe the pain of bankruptcy.
4. Banks suffer from bad debts.
5. Bankers become cautious about making new loans. They have more than enough trouble with bad debts on existing loans. The last thing they want is a bad debt on a new loan. Loan officers become afraid of jeopardizing their careers if they are not very cautious about new loans.
6. Both the demand for, and the supply of, new loans subside.
7. As bad debts multiply, banks may lack capital to make new loans.
8. As bad debts multiply further, banks have to call in existing loans because they have insufficient capital to support their current business.
9. Banks fail because the level of bad debts has wiped out their capital.
10. Depositors lose money as banks fail.

Meanwhile the money supply has progressively collapsed. Economic activity falls with it. The whole of the process is called debt deflation. The various stages of intensity should be noted. In the early 1930s the US reached stage (10), whereas the UK only reached stage (6) in the early 1990s.

Recapitulating, excessive monetary growth leads to asset-price inflation. Persistent asset-price inflation leads to a financial bubble in asset prices. The bubble bursts. Markets fall. The result becomes asymmetrical when the value of collateral in general falls below the loans being secured. Various degrees of debt deflation follow.

THE CURE FOR DEBT DEFLATION

Irving Fisher described debt deflation and its cure as long ago as 1932 (Fisher 1933). The money supply must not be allowed to decline when prices are falling. Money supply policy must be eased. But this advice needs interpreting for today's circumstances.

Some economists will misinterpret the advice straight away. They will confuse money supply policy with monetary policy. They will argue that lowering interest rates can be like pushing on a string and that nominal rates cannot fall below zero.

It is correct to argue that growth of the money supply can become inadequate if the only action taken by the monetary authorities is to lower interest rates. It is nevertheless wholly within the power of a government to ensure adequate growth of broad money. The government can boost the growth of broad money in the following ways. Listed in order of aggressiveness, it can:

- reduce the sales of its own debt, below that needed to cover its net cash requirement;
- buy back bonds that it has previously issued;
- extend the range of bonds which it buys, for example to include corporate bonds;
- extend the type of security, for example to include ordinary shares.

It should be stressed that it is wholly within a government's power to stop the growth of broad money from undershooting.

If a government underfunds in the way described, it prints money to replace fountain-pen money in decline. It allows people to sell assets to repay a bank loan without the money supply falling. It slows the downward spiral at its origin. People do not have either to sell assets or to reduce their expenditure on goods and services because they are unhappy about the amount of money in their bank account. Further, it helps directly to underpin asset prices and mutes the whole mechanism of debt deflation. It also helps banks to replenish capital as they enjoy profits in the bond market (for elaboration, see Pepper 1993: 36–8).

Easing fiscal policy can also boost the money supply, either by tax cuts or increases in public expenditure. This is the Keynesian remedy for debt deflation. (The resulting rise in the PSNCR boosts monetary growth, assuming that there are not any additional sales of public sector debt to the non-bank private sector.) There are two disadvantages with the Keynesian remedy. First, the result can be an increase in the National Debt to an unsustainable level and, in extreme cases, National Debt compounding out of control. Underfunding does not suffer from this disadvantage because any increase in the National Debt is backed by holdings of assets. Indeed, there is a good chance that underfunding, by purchasing ordinary shares, will turn out to be profitable in due course as capital profits are enjoyed when the stock market rebounds. The final result may well be a fall in the National Debt. Secondly, fiscal policy cannot be eased as quickly as debt management can be changed; there is a time lag between a decision to ease fiscal policy and the full effect on the public sector net cash requirement and hence on the money supply and the economy.

DEBT MANAGEMENT POLICY IN THE UK

In 1998 operational responsibility for debt management decisions was taken away from the Bank. This, presumably, was a decision by Gordon Brown, the new Chancellor of the Exchequer, but officials in the Treasury would have offered advice. Lawson's memoirs provide ample evidence that the Treasury did not understand the role of overfunding in the 1980s, with the strong implication that the Treasury does not understand underfunding either (Lawson 1992: 458–60). The *1999–2000 Debt Management Report* states that the formation of the Debt Management Office, distinct from the Treasury and the Bank, will complete 'the separation between monetary policy and cash and debt management policy' (HM Treasury 2000: 1). The separation is ironic at a time when there is a possibility that debt management may need to become a vital part of monetary policy. Congdon (2000: 1) has argued that it is an example of British officialdom doing 'something silly'. The Bank is in a weak position to argue about the transfer of responsibility because it is open to the accusation that it is trying to gain back some of the empire which it has lost; that is, it is pursuing a vested interest. The change in responsibility for debt management may be judged by economic historians to be a major blunder. The Chancellor should at the very least study Irving Fisher's paper on debt deflation.[31]

11. Summary and conclusions of Part II

The UK authorities can be seriously criticized for paying insufficient attention to the behaviour of bank lending to the private sector. The criticism is not that they failed to forecast bank lending, because it is notoriously difficult to predict. The criticism is that they failed to realize the significance of what was happening when it was known that bank lending had become either very buoyant or, conversely, sluggish. Buoyant bank lending was an important cause of the Barber boom in the early 1970s and the main cause of the Lawson boom in the late 1980s. Sluggish bank lending – that is, a minor dose of debt deflation – was the main cause of the depth of the recession in the early 1990s.

Discussing the Barber boom first, the growth of broad money (M4) shot up to 22 per cent in both 1972 and 1973, as described in Chapter 1. In nominal terms the increase over the two years was £15,414m. The main explanation of the increase was lax credit policy rather than easy fiscal policy. Bank and building society sterling lending (M4 lending) rose by no less than £11,482m over the period while the public sector net cash requirement amounted to £6,043m.

The role of bank lending was even clearer during the Lawson boom. In 1985 M4 grew by 13 per cent, or £25,874m in nominal terms. The PSNCR was £7,445m and M4 lending was £34,028m. By 1989 the growth of M4 had risen to 18 per cent, or £64,755m in nominal terms. The PSNCR had become a *repayment* of £9,282m and M4 lending had increased to no less than £88,927m. Credit was clearly the overwhelming driving force behind M4's buoyancy.[32]

The background to the deep recession in the early 1990s was a substantial fall in the growth of M4, to 4.6 per cent in 1993 or £23,791m in nominal terms. The explanation of the fall was *not* tighter fiscal policy because the PSNCR went from the repayment of £9,282m in 1989 to borrowing of no less than £42,690m in 1993. M4 lending was the dominant cause: it fell from £88,927m in 1989 to only £22,575m in 1993.

It must be appreciated that bank lending has two effects. The credit transaction is a one-off. The fountain-pen money that is created by the credit transaction has a continuing effect as the money passes from hand to hand and is spent. Although the UK authorities have accepted the need to control the supply of printing-press money, by limiting the public sector net cash requirement and ensuring that it is fully funded by sales of debt, they have not accepted the need to control fountain-pen money, neither the demand for it nor its supply.

There is an important lesson here for the future. Gordon Brown, the current Chancellor of the Exchequer, gave the 1999 Mais Lecture. In it he explained that it was the Bank's role to control inflation, by varying interest rates, and that strict control of the PSNCR would prevent interest rates from having to rise to an unacceptable level. During the questions that followed his lecture he was asked whether he would use fiscal policy if the economy were subject to an unexpected shock. He replied that he would allow the PSNCR to rise as revenue reduced in a recession and as unemployment benefits, and so on, rose – that is, he would allow the automatic fiscal stabilizer to operate – but he would not use *discretionary* fiscal policy. The implication is that variation in short-term interest rates is the only discretionary weapon that the authorities intend to employ to control nominal GDP.

This 'one-club policy' has been, and will be, widely criticized. When policy needs to be tight the sectors of the economy sensitive to high interest rates are hit especially severely. In particular, if high interest rates cause sterling to appreciate, manufacturing industry can be hit very badly while other sectors of the economy, such as financial services, escape.

The Monetary Policy Committee of the Bank has so far been operating in very benign circumstances. In the 1990s commodity prices fell as a result of debt deflation in Japan and the Asian Tiger economies. This held down product-price inflation in both the UK and the US. This is why the result of excessive monetary growth in both countries was asset-price inflation rather than product-price inflation. Circumstances will not stay benign forever. At some time in the future GDP is likely to develop major unwanted momentum, possibly because of an unexpected shock to the economy, an incorrect forecast, necessary action being delayed or the Committee bowing to political pressure. The interest rate weapon will then be exposed as inadequate.

What other weapons can be used? The regulation of fountain-pen money is an intractable problem. Overfunding should be used as an offset but it is only a short-term weapon. Even this weapon is not in play because debt management policy has been formally separated from monetary policy. Irrespective of overfunding, a clear conclusion is that the control of bank lending needs strengthening.

Another intractable problem is how to arrest asset-price inflation after momentum has been allowed to build up. As explained, real rates of interest for financial transactions can be very low or negative while real rates for expenditure on goods and services are high. The level of nominal rates needed to stop asset-price inflation would have a severe impact on the real economy. This problem is connected with the first intractable one because excessive growth of fountain-pen money is the usual cause of asset-price inflation.

One way of controlling bank lending and fountain-pen money would be to resort once again to quantitative controls on bank lending, but this would be a very retrograde step. It would restrict competition between banks. The UK has been down this route before. The inefficiencies and distortions eventually become unacceptable. It is not a long-term solution. In any case, given the current absence of exchange controls, business would be booked offshore. What is needed is a mechanism that restricts the growth of the banking system as a whole but not the freedom of an individual bank to compete with other banks.

Another way that has been recommended is to impose capital ratios on banks and vary the ratios according to economic circumstances. Indeed, there is a long history of ratios that were originally prudential ones that were later used for monetary control or, more accurately, to reinforce the Bank's control over interest rates. One of the difficulties here is that banks' capital can behave in a way that is erratic, reducing with bad debts and increasing with retained profits and new issues of capital. Capital ratios would have to be altered to offset changes in the capital of the banking sector as a whole. Further, prudential regulations are international by agreement and very complicated. It would be extremely difficult for one country to depart from international practice.

The only remaining solution is control of bank reserves; that is, monetary base control. This is considered in Part III.

POSTSCRIPT: PRAGMATIC MONETARISTS

There is one final point. Pragmatic monetarists were defined in the Introduction as economists who, as time has passed and practical experience has been gained, while still accepting the theory of monetary control, have concluded that the theory cannot be turned into working practice. These economists, including many in the Bank, have found it quite impossible to find which measure of the money supply to target, at what level any target should be set to provide the desired economic results, and how to achieve the target when it has been set.

The reply to pragmatic monetarists is first to agree that it may well be impossible to find a single measure of the money supply to target if the objective is to manage expectations. Secondly, to agree that it is difficult to control underlying monetary growth from the demand side. Mistakes are bound to be made and substantial variations in the money stock from the desired path are highly likely. The authors' solution is supply-side control.

PART III

Policy Solutions

12. Monetary base control

In his memoirs Lawson (1992:77) issued a 'reader's health warning' that MBC was 'mind-numbing gobbledygook' to the general reader. An alternative view is that it is common sense. Inflation will not be controlled unless there is financial discipline. There will not be financial discipline if the balance sheet of the banking sector as a whole is allowed to grow at an unsustainable rate. This is what control of the money supply is all about. Even more basic is the rate of growth of the central bank's own balance sheet. Advocates of MBC are merely arguing that the Bank of England should accept the discipline of limiting the growth of its own balance sheet. The saga that follows is extraordinary. It is not often in economic history that an institution can be accused of being emotional.

In the Introduction it was explained that Part I of this book could not be a detached historical account because Pepper was closely involved with events from the mid 1970s until the late 1980s. The degree of his involvement, including the role of the Greenwell *Monetary Bulletin*, was then described. The same applies to Part III. On three different occasions during this period, Pepper was engaged in the debate surrounding MBC.

The first occasion was when he advocated monetary base control for the UK in the *Monetary Bulletins*. The first of these was circulated in January 1977 and was followed by others in March 1979 and July 1979. These and other *Bulletins* attracted the attention of Margaret Thatcher (Pepper 1998: 22–3). This led Lawson (1992: 79–80) to observe: 'The most influential UK proponent of MBC (Monetary Base Control) was Gordon Pepper ... he had established a private line to Margaret Thatcher when she was Leader of the Opposition.'

Margaret Thatcher became Prime Minister in May 1979 and commissioned an inquiry into MBC almost straight away. The debate started in June 1979 with a paper, 'Monetary Base Control', from the Bank (Foot *et al.* 1979: 149–59). The Green Paper *Monetary Control*, to which reference was made in Part I, was published in March 1980. It was followed in September by a conference held at Church House, Westminster, the joint chairmen being Peter Middleton, representing the Treasury, and John Fforde, representing the Bank.[33] Howe announced the authorities' decision in November 1980. It was that the UK would not adopt MBC. The battle for a reliable system of monetary control had been lost.

The second time Pepper was drawn into the debate was when Lawson conducted another review of monetary policy, which included the possibility of MBC, shortly after becoming Chancellor in 1983. This one was held in private but his meetings with Pepper are described in his memoirs (Lawson 1992: 452). MBC was again rejected, the crucial factor being the hostility of the Bank.

Pepper was involved a third time in the debate about MBC after the failure of monetary control had led to the Lawson boom and rising inflation. He made three contributions: an IEA Inquiry in April 1989, an IEA Research Monograph in April 1990 and the City University's Mais Lecture in May 1990. The Bank's reaction to these indicated that its attitude had, if anything, become even more entrenched.

This book is the fourth occasion on which Pepper has advocated MBC. He is only too aware that he will be accused of 'flogging a dead horse' and of being exceedingly boring. There are three main reasons for raising the subject yet again. The first is the logic of the first two Parts of this book. Part I explained that the experiment during the 1980s was mainly an exercise in political monetarism and not control of the supply of money. Part II described the urgent need to find an efficient way of controlling bank lending and fountain-pen money, and argued that other solutions did not stand up to examination. The second reason is that one of the main explanations Howe gave in his memoirs for rejecting MBC is no longer valid. The third is that both the Governor and the Deputy Governor of the Bank have changed and it is possible that the Bank's attitude to MBC has mellowed.

Advocacy of MBC in the UK can be a lonely position. There is a danger of being branded an extremist. Neo-Keynesians find the demand-side approach to monetary control and control of the counterparts of broad money relatively easy to understand (although they disagree with it). They have far more difficulty with MBC. It appears to them to be an extreme form of monetarism. This is in fact not the case. The North American and Swiss schools of monetarism consider it to be mainstream.

A rigorous treatment of the subject of MBC would start with a review of the literature that has emanated from the North American and Swiss schools. It would then survey the UK literature, including all the contributions to the inquiry instituted by Margaret Thatcher, and so on. The result would be a long and highly technical paper, which would be indigestible for many people. Instead, the aim is the limited one of describing the essence of MBC and of addressing the more important objections that were raised during the various debates. Pepper readily admits that the details of his proposals have evolved over time as he has learnt from others. It is hoped that the account of the debates during the 1980s will at least be of interest to contemporary economic historians.

HISTORICAL BACKGROUND

The idea behind monetary base control is the old one of a central bank controlling the quantity of reserves available to banks. Banks need reserves to support their businesses. In the UK their most liquid assets are their vault cash (till money) and their balances with the Bank. Then used to come call money with a discount house, Treasury bills, commercial bills eligible for rediscount at the Bank, short-dated gilt-edged stock, and so on. Over the years there have been various definitions of reserves, namely 'cash', 'liquid assets' and 'reserve assets', depending largely on the liquidity of the assets included in the definition.

During the early days of banking, prudence determined the amount of the various types of reserve that banks kept relative to their deposits. Over time the ratios became formalized. The Bank then started using the ratios to assist monetary policy. At one time the London clearing banks were subject to an 8 per cent cash ratio and later more emphasis was placed on a 30 per cent liquidity ratio. During the CCC regime in the 1970s there was a 12 1/2 per cent reserve asset ratio. It should be noted that the Bank could control the quantity of neither liquid assets nor reserve assets because some of the assets so classified, for example call money with discount houses and commercial bills, could be manufactured by banks.

Early textbooks nevertheless often suggested that these ratios could be used to limit banks' ability to take deposits. Under the 8 per cent cash ratio, for example, if the authorities allowed cash to increase by £100m deposits could increase by £1,250m (8 per cent of 1,250 = 100). Under the 12 1/2 per cent reserve asset ratio, if reserve assets were allowed to increase by £100m deposits could increase by £800m (12 1/2 per cent of 800 = 100), and so on.

DEFINITIONS OF THE MONETARY BASE

Currently, attention is focused on two definitions of reserves, namely the narrow and wide monetary bases. The narrow monetary base is banks' most liquid reserves; that is, their vault cash plus their balances with the Bank (that is, the money on which banks depend, which is sometimes called high-powered money). The wide monetary base is the narrow definition plus notes and coin in circulation with the public. Note that all of the components are liabilities of the Bank (apart from coin, which is a very small item).[34] Note also that notes and coin that are in the hands of the public, rather than a bank, are not bank reserves.

At first sight the narrow definition of the monetary base appears to be the obvious one to use, because its components are all reserves for a bank. Banks can however increase the narrow monetary base if they can increase their holdings of vault cash by persuading the public to hold fewer notes and coin. The advantage of the wide definition is that it is wholly under the control of the Bank. Banks cannot manufacture it.

There is further complication. If the monetary base is to be used for control purposes there may or may not be a mandatory ratio.

In response to the various criticisms that have been raised during the debates, Pepper has come to the conclusion that it is better to use the wide definition of the monetary base and not to have a mandatory ratio. (A mandatory ratio for the narrow monetary base would be similar to the old 8 per cent cash ratio.) Some of the more important criticisms are discussed below, starting with those brought up during the debates and finishing with those specifically mentioned by Howe and Lawson.

CRITICISMS OF MBC

Criticism 1: MBC would be incompatible with the Bank's role of lender of last resort

The first answer to this criticism is that most financial crises occur after a financial bubble has been allowed to form, and this happens when banks are permitted to expand their balance sheets at an unsustainable rate. Because MBC is designed to prevent excessive growth of banks' balance sheets it should also stop major financial crises from occurring. Prevention is better than cure.

The second answer is that if, in spite of the above, a financial crisis does occur, the Bank's lender-of-last-resort role should have complete priority over MBC. A rise in the monetary base does not matter in such circumstances because the additional reserves will not be used, as confidence will be low. The additional reserves can be quietly mopped up when confidence returns.

Criticism 2: There would be a multiple contraction of banks' assets and liabilities if there were to be an unexpected downward fluctuation in the base

The first point to make is that no attempt should be made to control the monetary base by altering interest rates to influence banks' demand for reserves. If such an approach were to be adopted, the base would probably fluctuate all over the place, as happened in the US during the experiment controlling bank reserves in 1979–80 (see below). Unexpected downward fluctuations would then be highly likely. The approach to monetary base control should most certainly not be a demand-side one.

To ensure that unexpected downward fluctuations in the base do not occur, the base must be completely under the control of the Bank. This is the main reason why the wide definition of the base is to be preferred. The important feature is that its components comprise the bulk of the Bank's liabilities. *The Bank can control the total by managing the size of its balance sheet.* It can sell some of its assets (primarily, bills in the domestic money market or foreign currency in the foreign exchange market) if its balance sheet is growing too quickly. It can buy assets if its balance sheet is growing too slowly. Hence the assertion that advocates of MBC are merely arguing that the Bank should accept the discipline of limiting the growth of its own balance sheet.

The important difference in the money market is that the Bank would decide on what quantity of 'assistance' to give each day; it would not passively supply whatever quantity banks wanted.[35] *It would cease to be a lender of first resort (although it would continue to be a lender of last resort, as described above).*

The possibility remains that there could be unexpected fluctuations in the total of vault cash and balances with the Bank because of a change in the amount of notes and coin in circulation with the public. This is one of the reasons for not advocating a mandatory ratio. Without one, banks would not need to respond straight away to a fluctuation in their reserves.

Criticism 3: Control of the wide monetary base would lead to precise control of neither bank reserves, because of switching between vault cash and notes and coin in circulation with the public, nor the money stock, because of the lack of a mandatory ratio

The answer to this criticism is that a fundamental role of money is to act as a buffer between income and expenditure decisions. The amount of money in the economy must be allowed to fluctuate if it is to fulfil this role. Precise control of the money stock is undesirable. Fluctuations in the money stock that reverse within about six months have no significance for the economy. *A desirable mechanism is one that prevents progressive departures of the money stock from target rather than precise short-term control.* Short-term fluctuations are only a major drawback if a monetary target is being used for political purposes.

Criticism 4: MBC would lead to violent fluctuations in interest rates

The essence of MBC is indeed that the Bank should decide on the amount of assistance that it gives to the money market each day, by buying or selling bills (or repos), instead of controlling the price of the assistance. If quantity is controlled rather than price, prices are bound *in the short term* to fluctuate by more (but see Appendix 5). However, it should be emphasized that large fluctuations in rates over the medium term are far more disruptive to the real economy than short-term ones. One of the main advantages of MBC is that it should ensure that interest rates are altered by a sufficient amount to control the money stock and prevent inflation from rising. It should stop interest rates being altered by too little, too late, as has frequently happened in the past when a discretionary policy has been followed. It should prevent the large medium-term fluctuations in interest rates that have done so much damage.

Criticism 5: Bank reserves are small relative to notes and coin in circulation with the public; if the latter varies and the former has to offset, variations in bank reserves will have to be very large and this would lead to big fluctuations in interest rates

Banks' reserves are currently minimal. Under the present system the main cause of fluctuations in banks' balances with the Bank is errors in the authorities' forecasts of the Exchequer's cash flow during a day. Indeed, bankers used to tell Pepper that they would be able to dispense with reserves altogether if only the authorities would get their forecasts right! Under MBC banks would need to hold substantially greater reserves than is currently the case. Buffers should be built into the system. Banks should not only be encouraged to hold adequate reserves but should also profit from having excess reserves that can be passed to other banks when the system comes under pressure. Adequate buffers, and no mandatory ratio, should ensure that short-term fluctuations in interest rates are kept to an acceptable level.

Criticism 6: Under MBC banks would be less profitable because additional reserves would be required and the interest earned on the reserves would be lower than what is earned at present. This is seen by some to be a tax on the banking system. Their argument is, the lower the tax; the more efficient is the banking system[36]

A root cause of the Barber and Lawson booms was banks providing too high a proportion of credit (the result being excessive growth of fountain-pen money). A basic reason for the high proportion was that banks were able to offer extremely flexible packages. The corporate bond market, for example, could not compete (Pepper 1990a: Ch. 10). The flexibility of the packages offered by banks depended on the Bank being willing to act as lender of first resort. The suggestion is that the Bank did not charge the banks enough for the services that it provided to them, the result being an uneven playing field, giving an advantage to banks over non-banks. If the Bank ceases to be lender of first resort, banks will not be able to offer such flexible packages or will have to charge more for them. The result will be that they will not provide so high a proportion of credit. At any rate, a tax on the banking system would be preferable to the banks providing so much credit that inflation ensues.

HOWE'S REASONS FOR REJECTING MBC

Howe's description of the MBC debate in 1979–80 is on page 152 of his memoirs. It is given below in full:

> The study of monetary base control (MBC) surfaced in the following March (1980) in the form of a Green Paper. This option centred around the theory that the Bank of England could control the money supply directly by manipulating and targeting the small deposits held by the clearing banks at the Bank. These deposits were seen as the 'base' of the total deposits of banks. This MBC option, while energetically advocated by some British individuals – notably Gordon Pepper of the stockbroking firm W. Greenwell – was mainly pushed by American monetarists. The system did not, however, sit comfortably with British practice. In contrast to the United States, the UK institutional set-up made the monetary base an unreliable indicator of the monetary stock. In no way could it be established as the basis of a totally new policy, at a time of so much change and turbulence in other respects. It is worth remembering that the US Federal Reserve, at this time, had initiated under Paul Volcker an MBC system. This did reduce inflation but at the expense of fluctuating interest rates. Despite this, mainly thanks to Pepper's influence on her at this time, Margaret Thatcher was particularly keen on this idea. She was ever on the look-out for some more automatic method of monetary control that would – as she hoped – avoid or reduce the need to raise interest rates. Not surprisingly, this magic formula was never to be found.

There are five arguments here: (1) institutional differences between the US and the UK; (2) a distinction between use of M0 as an indicator and MBC; (3) a distinction between transitional problems at a critical time and the need to adjust to financial innovation; (4) the lessons from the Volcker experiment; and (5) whether MBC would lead to lower interest rates. The last two will be discussed later, because Lawson makes related points.

As far as the first is concerned, Howe was correct to argue that the UK's institutional set-up was different from that in the US. This was so in two respects. First, the Bank makes no attempt whatsoever to control bank reserves – it is a lender of first resort – as explained in detail in Appendix 3. One of the objectives of MBC is to change this and therefore it is not an argument against MBC. The other difference in 1980 was the existence of the combination of the discount market and four extremely powerful London clearing banks, namely Barclays, Lloyds, Midland and National Westminster. The Bank wanted the discount market to survive as a buffer between the government and the banks, and was afraid that it might not do so under MBC because small discount houses would have to compete with very large banks.

In more detail, there used to be two buffers between the government and banks. The first was the Bank, acting as banker to the government. The second was the discount market. To maintain the second buffer, the bulk of the Bank's open-market operations was conducted through the discount market and not directly with the banks. Discount houses were also given priority at the weekly Treasury bill issue. Supposedly in return for underwriting the issue, discount houses used to have an agreement that the clearing banks would not apply at the issue but would instead purchase bills in the market a few days later. The Bank thought that the second buffer was desirable because it was concerned about a possible danger if the government were to deal directly with banks. One body would then in effect be dealing with four bodies. The Bank feared that this would lead to a progressively closer relationship; to more directives from the government to banks; and, eventually, to nationalization of the London clearing banks.

This argument against MBC has been overtaken by events, with the demise of the discount market and the growth in competition between banks, from ex-building societies, foreign banks, telephone banking and Internet banking.

As far as Howe's second argument is concerned, he does not appear to have understood the difference between using M0 as a demand-determined indicator and MBC under which the monetary base (that is, M0 by another name) would be supply determined.

Howe's third argument against MBC was that a totally new policy could not be established 'at a time of so much change and turbulence in other respects'. First, it must be admitted that the transitional problems during a changeover to MBC would be quite severe. As explained, banks' demand for reserves would jump because the Bank would no longer be lender of first resort. This means that the new aggregate that the authorities had chosen to target would appear to go berserk. It would take a little while for the banks to find out what reserves they would need in the new circumstances. While this was happening, it would be impossible to judge the stance of monetary policy by the behaviour of the monetary base. Ironically, broad money would have to be used during the transitional period.

Alan Walters, although in favour of MBC, was concerned about these transitional problems and judged that the circumstances were too critical to risk a changeover in 1981 (Walters 1984: 309). As far as Pepper is aware, the transitional problems were never discussed in detail. The Bank appears to have blocked any discussion of them, presumably because it did not wish to concede the principle of MBC. *The important point is that the right time to change to MBC is when there is not a crisis.*

Secondly, critical circumstances should not be confused with turbulent behaviour of the monetary aggregates because of financial innovation. At a time of changes of this sort, it is wise to go back to first principles. A firm foundation for monetary policy would be laid if the Bank controlled the growth of its own balance sheet. Financial innovation is an argument *in favour* of MBC (see Pepper 1998: 24). (It is also an argument for not having varying reserve requirements for different types of deposit, as in the US, or else the base would become distorted as switching took place between the different types (Pepper 1990a: 61).)

Howe also refers to MBC on pages 485–6 of his memoirs. He reports that Margaret Thatcher on holiday in August 1980 discussed her 'monetary dismay' with Fritz Leutwiler, head of the Swiss Central Bank, and the monetary economist Karl Brunner, then of Rochester University, 'who responded by laying the blame quite simply upon the Bank of England, for its refusal to adopt the monetary-base method of controlling the money supply'. At the start of 1981 Alan Walters became the Prime Minister's Chief Economic Adviser and, in partnership with Alfred Sherman, commissioned Jürg Niehans, a distinguished Swiss monetary economist, to write a report on monetary policy for Mrs Thatcher (Niehans 1981), which she read in February 1981 (Thatcher 1993: 133–4). After five weeks' work, Niehans reported 'in favour of using the monetary base' (see Thatcher 1993: 133–4). The UK economists arguing for MBC had strong support from abroad, but to no avail.

LAWSON'S REASONS FOR REJECTING MBC

Lawson's description of the debate about MBC in 1979–80 is on pages 79–82 of his memoirs. Again, it is given below in full:

> The monetarist reformers wanted the Bank of England, instead of trying to influence the demand for money via interest rates, to control the supply of money more directly by setting a target for the banks' reserves with the Bank. They regarded these reserves as the 'base' of the much larger volume of bank deposits: hence the expression 'Monetary Base Control' or MBC. Although MBC enthusiasts sometimes skate over the issue, there can be no question of the Bank of England refusing to lend to the banks if they are short of reserves. For its task is to support the financial system – not to engineer its collapse – by acting as 'lender of last resort'. The MBC proposal, in its more realistic form, is that the Bank should let its lending rate to the money market rise or fall to whatever extent is required to keep bank reserves to a predetermined growth path.
>
> The most influential UK proponent of MBC was Gordon Pepper, then a partner in the stockbroking firm of W. Greenwell. Pepper had done highly useful work in translating the rarefied concepts of monetarist academics into actual day-to-day operations of the banking system. Then in his prime, he had established a private line to Margaret Thatcher when she was Leader of the Opposition. But like many such technical experts, he greatly exaggerated what could be achieved by institutional changes in financial mechanisms.
>
> The secret of his appeal to Margaret Thatcher was that he had persuaded her that a given degree of monetary tightness could, through MBC, be secured at an appreciably lower level of interest rates than the UK was experiencing. Given her – by no means unique – detestation of high interest rates, a promise of sufficient monetary tightness to bring down inflation at lower interest rates had an irresistible appeal.
>
> In fact real interest rates in 1980 were not particularly high – indeed, on the basis of headline inflation they were at times negative, decidedly so after allowing for tax. But they came as a shock compared with the rates prevailing during the financial year 1977–78, when real bank base rates averaged *minus 6 1/2 per cent* – a ludicrous figure, which if it had persisted would soon have secured Keynes's euthanasia of the *rentier*.
>
> Ironically, the US Federal Reserve under Paul Volcker had inaugurated a temporary experiment with a form of monetary base control in the autumn of 1979. The tight

money which it embodied did succeed in bringing down US inflation quickly, but interest rates fluctuated very sharply and were often very high; the interest rate on call money reached a peak of over 20 per cent in 1981, much higher than anything seen in the UK.

MBC in the UK was advocated in two forms: with or without a mandatory requirement for the banks to maintain given reserves at the Bank of England. If mandatory reserves exceeded the amount that banks wanted to hold voluntarily, they would act as a tax on them. But the result would simply be to redirect the lending via offshore subsidiaries outside the Bank's control. So I agreed with the Bank of England that a non-mandatory version was the only one worth considering.

There remain other problems with MBC, even if the Government is prepared to take the risk of large interest rate fluctuations. The biggest one is that the ratio of total deposits to reserves – the 'base multiplier' – may not be stable. Even slight variations in this multiplier would cause enormous variations in all the broader measures of the money stock. These unpredictable elements would have compounded the existing problem of the short-term instability of the demand for money. The Bank of England, which deeply disliked the whole idea of MBC, inevitably also raised many more technical problems connected with money market management.

Not surprisingly, the Green Paper was distinctly cool about MBC, although it did ask readers for views on whether 'the difficulties could be surmounted'. Given the problems we were experiencing with monetary control, I was personally attracted to the idea of MBC – although highly doubtful of its promise of lower interest rates for a given degree of monetary tightness. I also shared the suspicion that the Bank of England's root-and-branch opposition to MBC was at least in part because it would have meant the demise of that venerable top-hatted institution unique to the City of London, the Discount Market.

But I was in no doubt that to go to MBC would have been a leap in the dark for the authorities and the banks alike, with the risk of extraordinary interest rate volatility (as in the US), at least until the system settled down. I was also impressed by the fact that, apart from Switzerland, no country in the world had tried it out in practice; and the Swiss were before very long to drift away from it in practice in favour of loosely linking their currency to the Deutschmark. Above all I was convinced that such an experiment had a chance of success only if those responsible for its implementation wished to make it a success. Given the Bank's profound antipathy, it would all too likely have proved the disaster they predicted. Certainly the risk was too great to take.

Margaret Thatcher was deeply disappointed by this conclusion, and throughout her time in office, whenever interest rates had to rise significantly, her interest in MBC in some shape or form revived. It was encouraged from the beginning of 1981 onwards by Alan Walters, part of whose appeal to her was that he was usually in favour of lower interest rates (whether via MBC, of which he was an advocate, or by 'letting the pound find its own level' on the foreign exchange markets).

No serious advocate of MBC today believes that bank lending can be fine-tuned. The credit cycle is endemic and unpreventable: the practical question is how far can it be dampened. The early MBC enthusiasts claimed it was a sure means of monetary control, whereas interest rates were not. To which the practical man rightly replies: 'If MBC is so superior, why is it that nobody – not even the powerful and independent German Bundesbank – uses it?' The Bundesbank's so-called 'Minimum Reserve requirement' is *not* a means of directly controlling either bank lending or even the money stock. It is a seldom-used auxiliary means by which the Bundesbank generates the interest rate it believes necessary, as the Bundesbank itself has frequently explained.

> The 1980 Green Paper is still worth reading in the 1990s, not least because it punctures some perennially topical delusions. One of these concerns the use of some kind of reserve assets ratio – which has an attraction for Labour Party advisers, who see it as a form of direct control over credit. The Green Paper makes it clear that it is not, any more than the Bundesbank's Minimum Reserve requirement is. There was indeed a scheme by which the Bank of England could call on the banks to increase their deposits with it by a specific amount when it wanted to tighten credit, known as Special Deposits, which earned no interest. These were instituted in 1960, but were not as effective as intended because the banks could offset a call for them by bidding for funds in the wholesale money markets. The practical point, however, is that the Bank sought to use the scheme to raise interest rates, and not to control the money stock directly. (Lawson 1992: 79–82)

Lawson raises many points, some of which have already been answered. Of the remaining ones, four stand out: (1) the US experiment with control of bank reserves; (2) the Bank of England's entrenched attitude; (3) whether the level of interest rates would tend to be lower under MBC; and (4) the practice of other countries.

THE US EXPERIMENT

In the autumn of 1979 Paul Volcker had indeed announced that bank reserves would be controlled in the US. It transpired, however, that the chosen mechanism bore no resemblance to the textbook model of monetary base control or what has been advocated for the UK. Pepper had a meeting in Washington in 1980 with an official of the Federal Reserve System who described the *modus operandi* of the new method. Pepper could hardly believe his ears. He was told that the Fed had developed an equation for bank reserves and used it to forecast banks' demand for reserves. They then altered interest rates by the appropriate amount to bring banks' demand for reserves into line with the target for reserves. It was demand-side control of the monetary base! Because of the lag before changes in the Federal Funds rate affects banks' demand for reserves, the mechanism described appeared to Pepper to be unstable, and wild fluctuations in both interest rates and reserves could be expected. These did indeed occur but it eventually transpired that the mechanism was far more complicated than had been explained by the official. Poole (1982) gives an authoritative description, which is not reproduced here because it is very complicated for UK readers who are not knowledgeable about the US system.

The detail of the method of control employed in the US is not important for the purposes of this book because the plain fact of the matter is that the base was not controlled. The three month annualized rate of growth of the monetary base in the US went from 3 per cent to 12 per cent, to 2 per cent, to 5 per cent, to nil, and then to 12 per cent.[37] The experiment was clearly *not* with the type of monetary base control that has been advocated for the UK.

(A possible explanation of the peculiar method adopted by the Fed is that it may have been merely a political device to raise interest rates to a level that would not otherwise have been acceptable and to give a downward shock to inflationary expectations (Mishkin 1997: 492). If so, the experiment may be considered to have been a success because the secular upward trend in inflation was broken.)[38]

THE BANK'S ENTRENCHED ATTITUDE

Lawson's description of the Bank's attitude to MBC in his account of the 1979–80 review of MBC should be noticed. 'Deeply disliked', 'root-and-branch opposition' and 'profound antipathy' are strong words. Notice also his conclusion:

> Above all I was convinced that such an experiment had a chance of success only if those responsible for its implementation wished to make it a success. Given the Bank's profound antipathy, it would all too likely have proved the disaster they predicted. Certainly the risk was too great to take.

He also comments on three subsequent reviews of MBC:

> **Review in 1983 (when he became Chancellor)**
> The outcome of the review, which had of course been conducted in close collaboration with the Bank, was somewhat inconclusive. There was general disillusion with sterling M3, but no interest in Monetary Base Control. Here the Bank's *hostility*, coupled with the considered rejection in 1981, was decisive. Dissatisfied by the unsatisfactory nature of the outcome but still not entirely clear in my mind as to the best way ahead, I arranged a couple of private meetings in the summer of 1983 with Gordon Pepper, whom I had known for over a decade, and who was at that time the leading monetary analyst in the City.
>
> Pepper was scornful of broad money and favoured going over to Monetary Base Control (MBC). He knew, however, that the Bank, which would have to operate MBC, was very hostile to it; and agreed that in those circumstances to impose it on the Bank would be asking for trouble. (Lawson 1992: 452, emphasis added)
>
> **Seminar with Margaret Thatcher in 1985**
> At the second seminar, which was attended by Alan Walters, Margaret once again raised the issue of Monetary Base Control, which the Bank again found technically difficult. The issue was satisfactorily put to bed with the promise of 'further studies' of the US and German systems. (Lawson 1992: 480)
>
> **Criticism in 1989**
> The devices usually suggested had been aired for a very long time ... Although I did not share the Bank's *abhorrence* of MBC ... (Lawson 1992: 853, emphasis added)

The descriptions 'deeply disliked', 'root-and-branch opposition', 'profound antipathy', 'hostility' and 'abhorrence' describe an attitude to MBC that goes beyond the bounds of reasoned argument.

The Bank's response to the debate about MBC in the late 1980s showed that it remained extremely hostile. Tony Coleby was the Bank's Executive Director in charge of domestic monetary policy at the time of Pepper's Mais Lecture in 1990. He responded in a letter to Pepper, which was circulated quite widely, the conclusion of which was, 'I can find nothing in your paper of the slightest value to the conduct of policy'!

Part of the Bank's hostility to MBC was that of Keynesians to monetarism. Gordon Richardson was Governor from 1973 to 1983, when Robin Leigh-Pemberton (now Lord Kingsdown) succeeded him. A former colleague has said that Richardson was converted to monetarism but Leigh-Pemberton, surprisingly, never was.[39] The Deputy Governor, Kit McMahon, probably had a crucial role. Before he joined the Bank, McMahon had been a Fellow and Tutor in economics at Magdalen College, Oxford. He rose through the Bank's research department to become an Executive Director in 1970 and Deputy Governor between 1980 and 1988. He is an intellectual of considerable stature who was, and remains, a Keynesian. He has always been very hostile to monetarism.

Even given allowance for the Keynesian views of its officials, the emotional reaction of the Bank was unusual. There are various possible explanations. The first is that the Bank may have thought that MBC would restrict its role as lender of last resort. This is one of the basic functions of a central bank. As someone said during the debate, the threat of MBC was like placing a dagger close to the heart of the Bank. A second explanation was the desire to protect the discount market, mentioned by Lawson and already discussed. A third was that banks were definitely against MBC. There are many examples of a regulator becoming too close to the firms being regulated, with the result that the regulator eventually becomes encaptured by the industry it is meant to be regulating. Commercial banks have a strong vested interest in avoiding control of the money supply in general, because it implies a restriction on the growth of the banking sector as a whole, and control of bank reserves in particular, because it means greater competition. The suggestion is that the Bank may have allowed itself to be influenced too much by the arguments against MBC advanced by banks.

Remembering that MBC implies that a central bank should control the rate of growth of its own balance sheet, the Bank is, in spite of the above arguments, wide open to the accusation that, whereas it wants to impose discipline on others, it is not prepared to accept discipline itself.

Differences of Opinion within the Bank in the 1980s

The authors have been told that the attitude within the Bank during the MBC debates of the 1980s was not completely uniform.[40] Some, like Coleby, did find the idea 'abhorrent' but others thought that MBC might solve some of the difficulties with the existing method of monetary control. MBC might provide a solution but they thought that it could not be adopted without legislation and the Government did not appear to be willing to legislate.

In more detail, the argument was that to have tried to impose MBC using the 1979 Banking Supervision Act would have been defeated in the courts because it would not have been accepted as a purpose within the terms of that Act. The alternative of trying to impose it voluntarily would have been grossly unfair on any institution that did comply. Previous experience had shown that foreign banks and other financial institutions would not comply voluntarily. Non-compliers would have eagerly carried out the financial activities turned away by compliers. Although some in the Bank thought that MBC might be intellectually appealing, the conclusion was that it was just not practical without legislation.

It may be noted that the argument about legislation being necessary applies to MBC with a mandatory ratio. It is not clear that legislation would have been necessary for the sort of MBC advocated in this book, that is, without a mandatory ratio.

Dislike of Volatile Interest Rates

Another argument that helps to explain the attitude of the majority within the Bank is dislike of volatile interest rates. Most bureaucrats want markets to be orderly. The Bank's long history of trying to preserve an orderly gilt-edged market is an excellent illustration of this. Eddie George has, however, succeeded Leigh-Pemberton as Governor and is unusual because he is a market man. This is in sharp contrast to Richardson and the Earl of Cromer (who were merchant bankers) and Leigh-Pemberton (who was a clearing banker). From first-hand experience in the gilt-edged and foreign exchange markets, George is well aware of how official attempts to smooth market movements can encourage speculation and, in the long run, have exactly the opposite effect to that intended. He is also aware that a grossly disorderly market in the short run can lead to a much more stable market later on. George has, for example, masterminded some classic 'bear squeezes' in his time. In short, George is the first Governor not to be afraid of disorderly markets and is likely to attach less importance than his predecessors to short-run volatility of interest rates under MBC. Further, Mervyn King, the present Deputy Governor, is not a close-minded Keynesian. Now that both the Governor and the Deputy Governor have changed, the Bank's attitude to MBC may have mellowed.

LOWER LEVEL OF INTEREST RATES

Howe, Lawson and the Bank all challenge the argument that, for a given degree of monetary tightness, interest rates would be lower under MBC than under the current system of monetary control.

The first argument is a long-run one. A permanent reduction in interest rates depends on fighting inflation. Supply-side control of the money stock is a more reliable way of making certain that this battle is won because it is a surer way of preventing excessive monetary growth than demand-side control. Expectations should also help. The adoption of a more powerful method of control should reduce people's inflationary expectations. If this were the case the reduction in interest rates would be brought forward.

The second argument is more controversial. *It is that a rise in interest rates that is accompanied by a constraint on the supply of money and credit has a more powerful effect than a rise in interest rates in isolation.* This argument is in fact merely an extension of the one expressed at the start of Chapter 9. If the supply of money is greater than the demand for money, interest rates will fall but there will be a delay before the market clears and returns to equilibrium and, while this is happening, some of the excess money is likely to be spent. Expenditure on goods and services implies that availability of supply has a direct effect in the market for goods and services. Expenditure on existing assets implies that availability of supply has a direct effect in the market for financial assets. If the same applies in the market for bank reserves, the argument that interest rates would be lower under MBC is correct.

Rubbing home the theme, businessmen will agree that if goods are priced correctly but there is not much money around, sales will not be very buoyant. If there is a lot of money about but goods are priced expensively, sales will again not be very buoyant. Buoyant sales occur when there is a lot of money about and goods are priced correctly. Experienced stock market investors will agree that there will be a substantial rise in the stock market if an unexpected item of good news occurs at a time when there is a lot of money about; that is, if the financial institutions are flush with funds. If the same item of unexpected good news occurs at a time when there is little money about – that is, if the institutions are short of funds – the reaction of the market will be muted.

In both cases it should be stressed that the important factor is not availability of supply alone but the combination of abundant supply and attractive price.

Many economists will disagree that the combination of availability of supply and price can have a greater effect than price alone. Some will argue that MBC is merely a way of ensuring that interest rates are set at an appropriate level.[41] Coleby had a second conclusion in his letter responding to Pepper's Mais Lecture. It was that 'the notion of supply-side control operating independently of interest rates belongs only in the imagination'. But the real world is more complicated than many theories assume. The UK's financial system is usually in the process of moving from one state of disequilibrium to another. Note that the assertion is *not* that the UK economy is usually in the process of moving from one state of *equilibrium* to another state of *equilibrium* but from one state of *disequilibrium* to another state of *disequilibrium*. A lot of economists accept that markets often do not clear straight away – a change in price may not bring supply and demand into line quickly – and that supply can have a direct effect while a market is clearing, but they argue that this only lasts a short time. In the real world, though, some factor or other often changes before markets have had time to reach the new state of equilibrium. In the extreme, markets may never reach an equilibrium because something is always changing, and may be continuously trying to clear. Availability of supply can have a direct effect, not only for a short time but for most of the time.

THE PRACTICE OF OTHER COUNTRIES

Lawson was right to argue that Switzerland was the only country in 1990 that controlled its monetary base but he did not mention that the UK and Luxembourg were the only countries in the European Community not to have reserve requirements (Deutsche Bundesbank 1990: 21–8). It is also true that one of the purposes of a central bank having reserve or liquidity requirements is to influence interest rates. It may indeed be the main intention, but this book has argued that control of reserves has other effects.

Before the advent of the European Single Currency different countries placed different reliance on reserve ratios. The UK was at one end of the spectrum, with sole reliance on interest rates. The Swiss were at the opposite end, with sole reliance on control of bank reserves. Other countries were in the middle, with Germany close to the Swiss end. If it is correct to argue that a rise in interest rates combined with a constraint on the supply of money is more powerful than a rise in interest rates in isolation, the Swiss enjoyed full benefits, the Germans most of the benefits, other countries some of the benefits, and the UK none.

13. MBC versus funding policy

A classic example of the conditions in which availability of supply magnifies the effect of a change in the price of money was described in Chapter 10, when the cure of debt deflation was discussed. Many economists argue that monetary policy cannot be eased beyond a zero rate of interest, because rates cannot become negative. If the price of goods and services is falling, positive real interest rates, possibly high ones, cannot be avoided and the interest rate weapon has become ineffective. Chapter 10, in contrast, explained that, although growth of the money supply might easily continue to be inadequate if the only action taken by the authorities were to lower interest rates, it is wholly within the power of a government to ensure adequate growth of broad money by following a policy of underfunding. Buying back gilt-edged stock would offset a fall in the money supply as people sell assets to repay bank loans. People would not then have either to sell other assets or to reduce their expenditure on goods and services because they are unhappy about the small amount of money in their bank accounts. Such action to boost broad money would have a powerful effect on the economy in spite of it not being possible to reduce interest rates any further. In other words, supply of money would have an effect independent of price.

Monetary base control is an alternative to underfunding (or overfunding, as the case may be). How exactly would it work in conditions of debt deflation? As explained, the money supply would tend to fall as people sell assets to repay loans. This means that banks' liabilities would fall and their demand for reserves would decline in line. Under MBC, the Bank would maintain reserves at the old level. Banks' deposits with the Bank would accordingly become greater than banks want. A bank with surplus reserves would try to lend the unwanted reserves in the inter-bank market but this would merely pass the surplus to another bank. It would be like a game of pass-the-parcel. When the music stopped the bank holding the parcel would be left with the surplus deposit with the Bank.

Interest rates in the inter-bank market would tend to fall while this process continued but there would be little, or no, scope for a further decline in rates. A bank with surplus reserves would, before long and subject to the risk being acceptable, decide to purchase an asset on which the expected return is higher than that available in the inter-bank market; for example, a gilt-edged stock.

Under MBC, neither the Bank nor the government would be prepared to sell additional assets to banks, which would have to be purchased instead from the non-bank private sector (or from the overseas sector). The seller of the asset would receive a bank deposit in exchange. The result would be that banks' liabilities and assets would both rise, and their demand for reserves would increase in line. Banks would continue the process of purchasing assets for as long as they consider that the return on them is likely to be greater than that on a deposit with the Bank. They would also have an incentive to market and sell loans at very cheap rates, although fear of bad debts would damp their enthusiasm. Such acquisition of assets would continue until banks' demand for reserves had risen into line with the level maintained by the Bank.

(Coleby challenged the above in his letter to Pepper after the latter's Mais Lecture. He based his criticism on a detailed description of the way in which banks behave under the present system of monetary control, about which there was no disagreement. Unfortunately he did not distinguish between this and the way banks would behave if the Bank were no longer a lender of first resort. This failure to recognize the extent to which behaviour would change was one of the more depressing features of the debate about MBC.)

The overall effect of the process described above would be that banks would have purchased assets from the non-bank private sector instead of the Bank doing so under a regime of underfunding. Both actions would boost monetary growth. The advantages of MBC would be avoidance of the longer-term problems associated with either underfunding or overfunding, described in Chapter 8. Banks, acting in accordance with normal market criteria, rather than officials, would decide which assets to purchase. Pressure would not be confined to the gilt-edged market but would be spread across markets, including the money market.

MBC would also provide an incentive for banks to market and sell loans aggressively when reserves were in surplus and to moderate their activities when reserves were in short supply.

The position can be summarized succinctly. Monetary base control should, in addition to providing an incentive for banks to control their loans, privatize any residual need for the Bank of England either to underfund or to overfund. In extreme conditions it must be admitted that markets can cease to function; for example, banks may consider that the risks involved in purchasing assets are unacceptably high.[42] In such circumstances, market solutions are not effective and underfunding should be employed as a reserve weapon.

14. A published target for the monetary base

In the Introduction it was explained that the time lag between variations in monetary growth and the response of the economy is long and variable, and that understanding of the lag is insufficient to be able to fine tune the money supply – that is, to boost it in an attempt to minimize a recession and curtail its growth to minimize a boom – and that the best policy is to aim at steady monetary growth. This was the reason advanced for having a target for the money supply. There are other reasons (see Friedman 1962). One is that the existence of a target de-politicizes monetary policy. It helps, for example, to stop a government from organizing a pre-election boom in an attempt to win votes and from following popular short-run policies that are unsustainable in the longer run.

The argument for taking politics out of monetary policy has already been accepted with the delegation of operational decisions to the Monetary Policy Committee of the Bank of England but there is still the possibility that the Committee may bow to political or popular pressure. Further, the Committee may be influenced by the erroneous economic theories that were held by the 364 economists who wrote the infamous letter to *The Times* after the budget in March 1981. A target for a monetary aggregate that is proof against distortion, if one can be found in spite of the practical experience in the early 1980s, would be a more robust solution.

The monetary base is such an aggregate. The central bank is the sole ultimate supplier of liquidity to the banking sector. Its liabilities are unique. They cannot be manufactured. Further, if a non-mandatory system is adopted, distortions to the components of the money supply, caused for example by financial innovation, will not feed back into the monetary base (see page 70). In short, the monetary base is the least likely aggregate to be distorted. It is an aggregate on which it should be possible to rely. It should only be necessary to suspend a target for the base in extreme conditions; for example, if a lender-of-last-resort operation becomes necessary to avoid a systemic collapse in the banking system (see page 66), if markets cease to function (see page 80) or, possibly, a major external shock to the economy.[43]

A target for the monetary base has another advantage. Changes in interest rates would depend solely on market forces and not on action by the authorities. This would eliminate uncertainty caused by the authorities and the waste of resources spent Bank/Fed watching and trying to second-guess the authorities.

In more detail, with a target for inflation (or one for the exchange rate), interest rates are very largely administered by the authorities. Officials (at present the Monetary Policy Committee of the Bank, but in the past the Chancellor, after taking advice from the Treasury and the Bank) decide what interest rates to set. These prevail, subject to markets deciding that the ones chosen are compatible with acceptable objectives. Accordingly, anyone trying to estimate what interest rates are likely to do in the future has to pay a great deal of attention to likely actions by the authorities. A whole industry grows up watching the Bank and the Fed to detect clues about current thinking and subtle signals to markets. Will the authorities act this week or next? Will they do too little too late, as has happened so often in the past? Will politics or popular opinion intervene?

The situation would be very different under MBC. The operational details are very simple. The central bank merely controls the growth of its own balance sheet. As already explained, if the balance sheet is growing too quickly the central bank sells some assets, for example a bill in the domestic money market or foreign currency in the foreign exchange market. If its balance sheet is growing too slowly it purchases bills or foreign currency. *Interest rates and the foreign exchange rate are determined solely by market forces.* The markets would *know* that the monetary base would increase by a certain percentage each day. Uncertainty caused by the authorities would be eliminated.

15. Summary and conclusions of Part III

After showing in Part I that monetarism under Thatcher was an exercise in political monetarism rather than genuine monetarism, we provided a more detailed critique of monetary policy in the 1980s and 1990s in Part II, where the conclusion was that bank lending and fountain-pen money cannot be controlled by existing policy instruments. Part III has outlined the only remaining solution – monetary base control.

THE PROPOSAL

The wide monetary base should be controlled but there should not be a mandatory ratio for bank reserves. The wide definition consists of banks' deposits with the Bank of England and their vault cash, plus notes and coin in circulation with the public. With the exception of one small item these comprise the bulk of the Bank's liabilities.

THE ESSENCE OF MBC

Advocates of MBC merely argue that the Bank should accept the discipline of controlling the growth of its own balance sheet. Without such a discipline, monetary policy will not be based on a firm foundation. If its balance sheet is growing too quickly the Bank should sell some assets, for example a bill in the domestic money market or foreign currency in the foreign exchange market; it should buy assets if its balance sheet is growing too slowly.

OPERATIONAL CHANGES

The Bank should decide on the quantity of bills (and repos) in which it deals each day in the money market instead of dealing in whatever quantity of bills the banks want (albeit it at a price of the Bank's own choosing). In other words, the Bank should cease to be lender of first resort. Short-term interest rates would be determined by market forces instead of being administered by the Bank.

LENDER OF LAST RESORT

Financial crises usually occur after banks' balance sheets have been allowed to grow at a clearly unsustainable rate for many months. MBC would stop such growth from occurring and should, therefore, prevent financial crises. If one does occur in spite of this, lender-of-last-resort operations by the Bank should have complete priority over MBC.

PRECISENESS OF MONETARY CONTROL

Fluctuations in the growth of broad money that last for less than about six months have no significance for the economy. Precise monetary control is only desirable if a monetary target is being used for political purposes. A desirable mechanism is one that prevents progressive departures of the money stock from target rather than precise short-term control. MBC should do this.

INTEREST RATE FLUCTUATIONS

Interest rates will fluctuate more under MBC than under the present system. With no mandatory ratio for bank reserves, fluctuations should be kept to an acceptable level if sufficient buffers are built into the system. With the Bank no longer a lender of first resort, banks will need substantially larger reserves than at present. It should be stressed that large fluctuations in interest rates over the medium term are far more disruptive to the economy than short-term fluctuations. MBC should stop medium-term fluctuations from occurring because it would stop interest rates from being changed by too little, too late, as has happened so often in the past.

TRANSITIONAL PROBLEMS

Because banks would need additional reserves, the monetary base will increase rapidly during any changeover to MBC and the stance of policy will have to be judged temporarily by the behaviour of the other aggregates. Changeover in critical circumstances might be dangerous. The time for change is when conditions are stable. Ironically, this is when there is minimum pressure for change.

MONETARY TARGETS AND DISTORTIONS TO MONETARY AGGREGATES

One great advantage of a monetary target is that it de-politicizes monetary policy. The wide monetary base is the best aggregate to target because it is the aggregate least prone to distortion. This is because its components are liabilities of the Bank and cannot be manufactured.

REMOVAL OF UNCERTAINTY CREATED BY THE AUTHORITIES

Under MBC markets would know that the monetary base would increase by a certain percentage each day. Changes in interest rates would depend solely on market forces and not on action by the authorities. This would eliminate uncertainty caused by the authorities and the waste of resources spent Bank/Fed watching and trying to second-guess the authorities.

BANK LENDING

MBC would exert some direct influence on bank lending. Automatic overfunding or underfunding would occur to offset the behaviour of bank lending. Pressure would be spread across markets and assets, and asset allocation would be determined by normal market criteria instead of being administered by officials.

CONTROVERSIAL ASSERTION

Many economists accept that markets often do not clear quickly; that a financial system can be in the process of changing from one state of equilibrium to another; and that while it is doing so availability of supply can have a direct effect. The new state of equilibrium is, however, often never achieved because something changes before it is reached. In practice the UK financial system is usually in the process of changing from one state of *disequilibrium* to another state of *disequilibrium*, in which case availability of supply can have a continuous effect. The controversial assertion in this book is that an increase in the price of money – that is, in interest rates – combined with a constraint on the availability of supply, has a larger effect than an increase in interest rates in isolation. If this is correct MBC is not merely a system of monetary control that would stand up to pressure, but control could also be achieved at a lower level of interest rates than under the present system in the UK.

CONCLUSION

The overall conclusion is that, if the UK does not become a member of the European Single Currency, the debate about monetary base control should be reopened.

The authors issue a challenge to people disagreeing with this conclusion, of whom there will be many. It is for them to propose an alternative way of controlling bank lending, or offsetting fluctuations in it, that would be robust.

Appendix 1: Definitions of monetary aggregates

In order of broadness, starting with the narrowest, the aggregates are:

- Notes and coin in circulation with the public.
- M1 – notes and coin plus current accounts and sight deposits with banks denominated in sterling.
- M2 – M1 plus sterling deposit accounts and term deposits with banks, but excluding very large ones.
- M3 – M1 plus all sterling deposit accounts and term deposits with banks and certificates of deposit (CDs).
- M4 – includes sterling deposits with building societies as well as banks.
- M5 – M4 plus various other highly liquid sterling instruments, such as commercial bills.

In the interest of simplicity some detail has been omitted. The names of the aggregates and the precise definitions have changed over time. M3, for example, originally included foreign currency deposits. Publication of sterling M3 started in 1977 and it became the focus of attention because it omitted foreign currency deposits. Sterling M3 and M3 were renamed M3 and M3c in 1987. In 1988 attention switched from the new M3 to M4 because banks and building societies had become similar.

Appendix 2: The behaviour of broad money in 1980/81

The target for sterling M3 in 1980/81 was 7–11 per cent but its growth during the twelve months ending in December 1980 was 20 per cent; that is, it was running at a rate exceeding the upper limit of its target range by no less than 9 per cent. Howe ignored it and reduced interest rates. The result was a public relations disaster for monetarism. Walters returned to London in January 1981 to be the Prime Minister's economic adviser and, to many people's surprise and in spite of the behaviour of sterling M3, promptly declared that monetary policy was too tight rather than too loose.

Table A2.1 is designed to give an insight into what was happening to *underlying* monetary growth at the time. It shows the growth of the various aggregates during the twelve months ending in December 1980.

A2.1 Growth of monetary aggregates, December 1979–December 1980

M0	5%
Retail M1[44]	3%
Sterling M3	20%
M5	13%

Source: Greenwell (1981), Pepper (1990a: 39).

As explained earlier, sterling M3 was distorted upward during the period by:

- The unwinding of the bill leak to circumvent the 'corset'.
- The unwinding of the euro leak to circumvent the 'corset' after exchange controls were abolished.[45]
- Competition between banks and building societies, with banks gaining market share.

M5 allowed for the first and last of the above distortions. It will be seen that its growth rate was 13 per cent compared with 20 per cent for sterling M3. The upward distortion to M5 from the euro leak could not be estimated. All that could be said for certain was that the growth of broad money above the upper limit of its target range was less than 2 per cent.

Two other factors should be noted. The first is the sluggish behaviour of the narrow aggregates. This was especially significant as interest rates had been reduced, which should have given narrow money an upward boost because people had less incentive to switch into interest-bearing deposits. The underlying demand for transactions was likely to be even more sluggish than the data suggested. The second was that the pattern of relative interest rates suggested that many people would be very happy to leave their savings on deposit with a bank. Interest rates were higher than the rate of inflation. They also fell as the term of an investment increased. This meant that the rate of interest on bank deposits was attractive and closest to the highest available in the market. The conclusion was that the savings demand for money was likely to be unusually high and rapid growth of broad money did not indicate inflationary pressure.

Pepper had in fact been arguing on the above lines since May 1980 that policy was too tight (Greenwell 1980). Walters, who pays a lot of attention to the behaviour of M0, records that he had said at a seminar and briefing in the US in October and November 1980 that he judged monetary policy to be too tight (Walters 1986: 145). Congdon, who attached little importance to the behaviour of narrow money, argued on rather different grounds after the worst of the post-corset distortions were over. His conclusion was:

> The increase in sterling M3 in the three months to November [1980], a period relatively free from post-corset adjustment, was at an annual rate of nearly 20%. Against this background, is it reasonable to expect inflation to continue falling? Isn't the credibility of the government's whole macro-economic strategy in doubt? The difficulty with this bearish argument is that even the most doctrinaire monetarists regard a revival in economic activity as a necessary link in the causal chain between money and inflation. There is at present no convincing evidence of such a revival. (Congdon 1981)

The conclusions of monetary economists who monitored the situation closely were very different from the impression given by the behaviour of the published data for sterling M3 relative to its target.[46]

Appendix 3: UK versus US monetarism

Both this Appendix and the next will seem very strange to many US economists. The reason is that the UK's current system of monetary control has been and remains very different from that in the US and from the descriptions in many textbooks. The Bank of England makes no attempt at all to control the quantity of bank reserves. The Bank is an openly declared and unlimited lender of first resort (albeit at a rate of interest of its own choosing). Since 1981 the UK has not had any reserve requirements for banks. *US criticism of the UK should be focused on the method of monetary control in the UK and not on monetary analysis that assumes the UK's existing system of monetary control.*

The Bank's chosen method of monetary control (assuming the money supply is to be controlled) is to alter interest rates to bring people's demand for money into line with the target for the money supply, or, more precisely, the target for the stock of money. It is a demand-side approach to controlling the money stock. The Bank does not attempt to control the supply of money directly. The Bank's various devices, for example the power to call for special deposits, are intended merely to reinforce its control over interest rates and, as a result, over the demand for money, as explained in Chapter 1.

If reserves were controlled by the Bank, monetary analysis would start with their behaviour, as is commonly the case in the US. Because the approach is demand side, analysis in the UK starts a stage earlier. The counterparts of broad money (M3 and M4, see Chapter 7) are scrutinized to ascertain the reasons for broad money's behaviour. Excessive growth may, for example, be due to an increase in either printing-press or fountain-pen money. If the former, the explanation may be a rise in public expenditure, a shortfall in public revenue or inadequate sales of public sector debt outside the banking sector. If the latter, borrowing may be by either the corporate or personal sectors. If it is by the corporate sector, the borrowing may be by either financial or commercial companies. All this is useful information for understanding what is happening within the financial system. Indeed, such analysis can be used in the UK to try to predict the future behaviour of broad money.

Because of the Bank's method of monetary control, there is two-way causality between the economy and the stock of broad money in the UK, with causality running from the economy to broad money and from broad money back to the economy, as explained in Appendix 4. The system is dynamic.

Further, the time lag between the economy and the response of broad money in the UK may at times be more stable than that between broad money and the economy. Pepper has even tried to predict monetary growth from the phase of the business cycle, although he admits it was trying to be too clever by half. This may seem heresy to some US monetary economists but it does not detract from the importance of variations of monetary growth for the future behaviour of the economy.

As was mentioned in Chapter 5, Friedman was very critical about the suggestion that a change in fiscal policy was one of the weapons to control the growth of broad money in the UK. Whereas it is correct to argue that there is no simple correlation between broad money and the PSNCR, *discretionary* changes in fiscal policy do have an impact on broad money (see Chapter 7).

Appendix 4: A monetary model for the UK

The UK's financial system is usually in the process of moving from one state of disequilibrium to another. It is rarely in equilibrium. The real world is more complicated than many economic theories assume. Markets, for example, often do not clear straight away; that is, a change in price may not bring supply and demand into line quickly. Availability of supply can have an effect independent of price.

THE NARROW AGGREGATES

M0 is a composite aggregate. It consists of notes and coin in circulation with the public, plus cash held by banks and banks' balances with the Bank. It is therefore in part a measure of liquidity in the private sector and in part a measure of that in the banking sector. It has two names: M0 and monetary base. Because the aggregate is merely used as an indicator in the UK it is usually called M0.

M0's characteristics depend crucially on the system of monetary control. Under the UK's current system, M0 is determined very largely by the demand for it and not by its supply, as would be the case if the monetary base were controlled directly. Extending the theme in Appendix 3, under the UK's current system the main causality runs from the economy to M0 and not from M0 to the economy. *Failure to appreciate this has led to much confusion.*

Because M0 is largely demand determined it might be thought that it would be merely a coincidental indicator of the UK economy, but this is not so. M0's largest component is notes and coin in circulation with the public and, as a result, M0 is influenced mainly by the behaviour of retail sales. Retail sales are, in turn, a leading indicator of the economy in the sense that if they grow at an unsustainable rate there will be inflation or a problem with the balance of payments, or both. M0 is, therefore, also a leading indicator.[47]

The next broadest monetary aggregate is M1, which consists of notes and coin in circulation with the public plus current accounts and sight deposits with banks. M1 too is largely demand determined because many people have deposit accounts with their banks and can transfer balances between current and deposit accounts when they so wish. If their current accounts are lower than the desired level they transfer money out of their deposit accounts and if their current accounts are higher they transfer money into their deposit accounts. This has infinitesimal effect on the economy, remembering that the UK does not have different reserve requirements for sight and term deposits.

There are, however, a small number of people who do not have an account with either a bank or a building society. Others do not have a deposit account as well as a current account. Even if they do, probably only a few have arrangements with their banks to transfer funds automatically between accounts to maintain a constant balance on their current account. If they do not have such an arrangement they have to make a conscious decision to transfer money from their deposit account to their current account when the balance on the latter falls below the desired level. They may well take the need to make such a transfer as an indication that they are overspending. Small businesses, in particular, pay great attention to monitoring cash flow. As well as making a transfer from a deposit account, people may decide to cut back on expenditure, with consequential effects on the economy.

One of the essential roles of money is to act as a buffer bridging the interval of time between expenditure being incurred and income being received in an uncertain world. This applies to narrow as well as to broad money. The level of money that an individual holds is often different from the ultimately desired balance. It will be larger if income is either higher or has been received sooner than expected, or if expenditure has been delayed or is lower than expected. Conversely, it will be lower if expenditure has occurred sooner than expected or if income has been delayed, and so on. The person will subsequently take action to restore his or her money balance to the desired level. At any point in time, many people will be in the process of adjusting their monetary positions towards their desired balance. There are lags in the adjustment process and while they are taking place narrow money is partly supply determined.

The above argument does not imply that changes in narrow money or M0 *cause* changes in expenditure. Narrow money is merely behaving as a pressure gauge. A barometer, for example, reflects a phenomenon that precedes bad weather; it does not cause the weather. One statistic can be a leading indicator of another without there being a causal relationship between the two.

BROAD MONEY

The crucial difference between broad and narrow money is that changes in broad money, and liquidity, can *cause* changes in economic activity and inflation.

The first point to make is that the supply of broad money is not always equal to the demand for it; that is, the market in money may not be in equilibrium. If the supply of broad money is in surplus, the price of money – that is, interest rates – will tend to fall but this is unlikely to bring supply into line with demand quickly; see below. In the meantime, the excess money can be spent in four ways:

- On goods and services, in which case economic activity accelerates.
- In a way that directly raises the price of goods and services – for example, on a commodity – in which case inflation rises.
- On non-sterling assets – for example, sterling deposits may be exchanged for dollar ones – in which case sterling tends to fall.
- On domestic assets, in which case stock market and property prices tend to rise and the change in wealth in due course affects economic activity.

The factors determining the supply of money will be analysed before those determining the demand for money.

The Supply of Broad Money

The supply of broad money depends in the short run on what is happening in the market for credit. The credit market may well be out of equilibrium, with the demand for finance in the economy as a whole not equal to the supply of saving. When this happens banks act as a buffer; that is, they are the residual source of credit for both government and industry. If the government does not succeed in raising all the finance that it needs in the gilt-edged market and from other non-bank sources, the remainder is automatically borrowed from the banks, at least in the short run. When industry's internal cash flow is inadequate to finance stocks (inventories) and fixed investment, and if industry does not obtain the remainder through the stock market, and so on, companies tend to use their overdraft facilities and credit lines with banks. Therefore, when the demand for credit begins to exceed its supply, both industry and government begin to borrow on a large scale from banks.

It should be stressed that banks cannot in the short run control the total of their holdings of assets because their customers, rather than the banks themselves, determine the take-up of overdraft facilities and credit lines. Banks have also only a little direct influence on the amount that the government borrows from them.[48] With customers and the government very largely determining banks' total holdings of assets, banks bid for the necessary funds to finance these holdings. This determines the level of bank deposits and hence the stock of money.[49]

Recapitulating, in the short run changes in the *money stock* depend crucially on imbalances between the supply and demand for *credit* in the economy outside the banking sector. *In this sense*, the *supply* of broad money depends on what is happening in the market for credit.

Changes in the level of interest rates affect both the supply of credit and the demand for it. They may be administered by the Bank or left to market forces.

Either way, interest rates are not the only factor determining the supply of savings and the demand for finance in the economy as a whole. Changes in interest rates arising from market forces tend to bring supply and demand into line but imbalances in the market for credit can persist for some time, even if the other factors affecting the demand and supply of credit remain unchanged. In practice the other factors are unlikely to remain unchanged. The result is that the market for credit is usually moving from one state of disequilibrium to another, with the current extent of disequilibrium determining the supply of money.

The Demand for Broad Money

The factors determining the demand for broad money in the economy as a whole depend on the purposes for which it is held. There are two main ones. Money is held to facilitate transactions and as a medium for savings.

The primary determinant of the demand for money for transactions purposes is the behaviour of national income, but the *level* of interest rates on bank deposits also has an influence. As far as the primary determinant is concerned, the demand for money rises both as real economic activity increases and with inflation. The effect of changes in interest rates is a little more complicated. Money for transactions purposes tends to be held in non-interest-bearing or low-interest-bearing deposits; that is, in mainly narrow money. The demand for these falls as interest rates increase, as people exchange these deposits for ones on which the full rate of interest is paid, as already explained. The transfers are, however, merely from one sort of deposit to another, from deposits held for transactions purposes to ones held as savings. Broad money is not directly affected, because it includes both types of deposit.

The main determinants of the demand for money for saving purposes are wealth and the merit of bank deposits as an investment relative to the alternatives available. The latter depends on how the rate of interest on bank deposits compares with the expected return on other assets, after taking risk into account. The important factor is *relative* interest rates rather than their *level.*

Summarizing, money is held for two main purposes: to facilitate transactions and as a medium for savings. The part that is held for transactions purposes is determined largely by demand. The remainder of the money stock is determined largely by supply. The system is out of equilibrium if the remainder is not equal to the demand for money for savings.

Disequilibrium

Continuing the analysis, any surplus money in the remainder can be: (1) unintended savings, or (2) intended savings but with savers unhappy about the rate of return on bank deposits relative to the expected return available on other investments.

If the deposits are unintended savings, economic activity will rise as they are spent and in due course product-price inflation may rise.

If the deposits are intended savings but savers are unhappy about the return on them, savers will switch out of these deposits into other assets. The result will be asset-price inflation. The rise in asset prices will in due course stimulate the economy, as wealth and confidence rise, and product-price inflation will follow if corrective action is not taken. It should be noted that in the case of savers being unhappy about the return on bank deposits, the time lag between monetary growth and the response of economic activity would be longer than usual, as happened in the 1980s.

If savers are happy with the level of bank deposits they are holding as savings, the system will be in equilibrium but only for as long as the pattern of relative expected returns remains unchanged. Any change in relative expected returns will upset the equilibrium, with consequential effects on the economy.

Appendix 5: Demand-side or supply-side control – speed of response of demand and supply

Consider first a market for a commodity in which either the supply or the demand responds quickly to a change in price. Suppose that supply and demand are equal at the current price but that either the one or the other subsequently alters. The price will rapidly change to a new level at which supply and demand will again be equalized. Everyone who wished to buy or sell at the new price would be able to do so. In technical language, the market will clear.

Contrast this with the market for a second commodity for which neither the supply nor the demand responds quickly to a change in price. Suppose that the market for this second commodity is in equilibrium at the current price but that subsequently either supply or demand alters. The market will not clear again at once. If demand has increased, the price will rise but this will not quickly encourage additional supply, or discourage the increase in demand unless the rise in price is extreme. Stocks will fall and someone who wished to buy at the ruling price may be told by a supplier that stocks have run out – that is to say, the buyer must wait for a new delivery. If supply has increased, the price will fall but this will not quickly encourage additional demand or discourage the increase in supply and stocks will rise.

Suppose that the authorities wish to control the total amount of the second type of commodity in existence. They can try to do so by controlling either supply or demand. They can, first, attempt to control demand by continuously varying the price, but the quantity will behave erratically because demand responds only slowly to price changes. If the authorities persist with the policy, the quantity will eventually be controlled but the fluctuations in the commodity's price may be large, *especially if the supply alters unexpectedly because of a non-price factor*.

The second way for the authorities to control the quantity of the second type of commodity is to control its supply. The total of the commodity in existence will be far more stable than under the first method. This does not imply suppression of the price mechanism. The price will fluctuate as demand changes. However, as erratic fluctuations in supply will be controlled at source, fluctuations in price because of unexpected variations in supply will not occur and the resulting ones may well be smaller than if control were via demand, especially if adequate stocks were held. This suggests strongly that control of supply is more efficient than control of demand if a commodity is of the second type.

Money is clearly a commodity of the second type. Neither the demand nor the supply of money responds quickly to changes in its price; that is, to a change in interest rates. The efficient method of controlling the amount of money in existence is, therefore, control of supply rather than control of demand.

Notes

1. Fortunately, a lack of 'official' evidence has not deterred the political scientists from examining the UK's monetarist experiment. Here, new theoretical developments have prompted political scientists to focus on the role of the policy experts, institutions and politicians in the policy-making process. This literature has been particularly exciting for those who wish to raise wider questions, and has been applied with limited success to the evolution of monetarism in the UK from the mid 1970s (Hall 1993; Oliver 1997).
2. Two examples will suffice. First, Geoffrey Wood has argued that the erratic movements in the velocity of circulation over the 1980s due to financial innovation had been recognized in pre-econometric-based versions of the quantity theory developed by Hume and Thornton. Although financial innovation might have unsettled some monetarist supporters, it did not 'discredit the quantity theory' (Wood 1995: 110) or disprove monetarism. Second, the challenges to Friedman and Schwartz's (1982) study – which showed that money was related in a stable way to income – by Hendry and Ericsson (1983) were rebutted by Holly and Longbottom (1985), who used the same econometric methods as Hendry and Ericsson. Undeterred, Hendry and Ericsson (1991) pursued further econometric tests on one of the equations used by Friedman and Schwartz and still rejected the arguments of the monetarists. In a reply, Friedman and Schwartz (1991) argued that the one regression on which Hendry and Ericsson had concentrated could not support an anti-monetarist conclusion and, if anything, tended to support the monetarist case. Both examples are highlighted to show that the claims made by Healey are open to many interpretations but do not explain the abandonment of monetarism in the UK.
3. Lawson (1992: 80) describes how Pepper had established a private line to Margaret Thatcher when she was Leader of the Opposition.
4. Pepper must admit a personal bias. A very early lesson he was taught in the gilt-edged market was 'ignore what central bankers say; watch what central banks do'. As a result he has always been sceptical about attempts to manage expectations in financial markets.
5. In a letter to the authors.
6. The Bank used to be perceived as all-powerful but greater expertise among brokers and investors meant that the Bank was increasingly being

challenged. An important reason why the policy was changed was that the Bank was losing too much money.

7. A seminar on 'Competition and Credit Control' organized by the Money Study Group, SSRC, held at the Bank of England on 15 June 1971; some of the papers were reproduced in *Bankers' Magazine*, September 1971.
8. Discount houses were subject to an 'undefined asset ratio' that might have been used to limit their holdings of CDs.
9. There were occasions when investors judged the Government's economic policy to be permissive and became reluctant to purchase new issues of gilt-edged stock. Sales of public sector debt to the non-bank private sector fell; the money supply rose; and investors became even more convinced that policy was permissive.
10. The Bank only considered M3 to be important and not DCE. DCE has had an unfortunate history in the UK. It was introduced by an unwilling Bank and Treasury at the instigation of the IMF in 1969 but was gradually removed from prominence after April 1971 when the IMF-imposed DCE limits came to an end. It should be noted that neither the Bank nor the Treasury has ever published a serious discussion of the monetary approach to the balance of payments, as formulated by IMF economists or by academic monetarists.
11. If a Treasury bill issue was ever to be under-subscribed the banks' balances with the Bank would rise and the government would have got its money interest free!
12. Congdon (1992: 209–34) gives a detailed description of 'British monetarism', including control of the 'counterparts' of M3.
13. Supporters of rational expectations argued that the length of time before inflation was brought under control would be determined by the speed with which individuals and institutions adjusted their expectations of future rates of inflation downwards, which in turn was connected to the credibility of the monetary authority. For the proponents of this theory, a sudden change in policy regime can be damaging if the regime has little credibility (Sargent 1993). For Matthews and Minford (1987: 62), the disinflation at the start of the 1980s was severe and 'expectations were quite unprepared for it'. Moreover, for supporters of rational expectations, an important influence on credibility is the growth path of government debt. Although there was a tight monetary policy in the early 1980s, there were big fiscal deficits which were being financed by borrowing at high nominal interest rates. As Leslie (1993: 69) explains, 'consequently, agents formed the view that the deficits would be monetized some time in the future and this view led to high current inflation – despite the severe recession'. These views are not discussed in this book.

14. According to the annual surveys of investment analysts by Continental Illinois, which were the most authoritative at the time, Pepper was the leading gilt-edged analyst from 1972 to 1981 and was often described as the guru of the gilt-edged market. As explained in the Introduction, the authorities thought him important because of the effect he could have on expectations. Middleton made it his business to get to know him well. The briefings that were non-attributable at the time, about the Green Paper *Monetary Control* and the MTFS, were in fact given by Middleton to Pepper.
15. In a non-attributable conversation with the authors.
16. Margaret Thatcher shared this conviction. In a memorable moment of her speech as Leader of the Opposition, to the Conservative Party Conference in 1978, when some Conservative backbenchers and members of the Shadow Cabinet were arguing that policy should be eased, she urged Prime Minister Callaghan 'to keep on taking the tablets, Moses'.
17. In correspondence with the authors about this book.
18. According to a non-attributable conversation with a senior ex-civil servant.
19. Lawson's terminology, more precisely a rate of price change, or an inflation, objective.
20. In correspondence with the authors about this book.
21. It is interesting to note that Lawson was in favour of ERM but against European Monetary Union (EMU); he did not appreciate how ERM would lead to EMU. Howe was pro both ERM and EMU.
22. The leading advocate of a nominal GDP objective was Lawson's close friend, Samuel Brittan, who argued for it repeatedly in the *Financial Times*. Lawson did not adopt it because he thought it to be too far removed from the instruments that the policy maker has at his or her disposal and from the information available to him or her, data only being available two to three months after the end of the quarter to which they refer and then subject to revision.
23. A reply is that an official's loyalty is to his or her minister and not the Prime Minister (Lawson 1992: 486).
24. In correspondence with the authors about this book.
25. See note 14.
26. The falsehoods described are involuntary ones. It might be thought that officials would try to avoid them whenever possible but there is even a danger that involuntary falsehoods that are perceived to be in the national interest can become voluntary ones. Pepper was upset on one occasion when a very senior civil servant, for whom he had previously had great respect, volunteered a falsehood at a private function in someone's home. (The only alternative interpretation was that the official was either ignorant or stupid, which he was not.) The civil servant brought up the subject and

misled Pepper, apparently deliberately. The point of telling this story is not to accuse the civil servant of behaving in a dishonourable way but to report the reaction of someone equally as senior when told the story several years later. The second official did not challenge the story or express surprise, confirming the length to which some officials are prepared to go to spread misinformation.

27. Lawson gives another example of deception in his memoirs. In August 1981 MLR (the old Bank Rate) was abolished. Instead, short-term lending to the money market by the Bank was made within an undisclosed band. This band determined base rates; that is, the rate on which bank overdrafts are based. The main point of the change was to de-politicize interest rate changes. It was more apparent than real because the Government still initiated interest changes via the Bank. As Lawson (1992: 85) states, 'the supposed experiment was a particularly transparent smokescreen'.
28. Alternatively, the bank may place the money on call with a discount house, which will buy the Treasury bills.
29. Lawson was not the only person who believed that overfunding was essentially a way of massaging the money numbers. Insofar as others agreed with him, the published data for monetary growth did not reduce inflationary expectations by the amount they should have done.
30. According to the efficient-market hypothesis causality runs from changes in expectations to movements in share prices. Here it is argued that causality runs the other way; that is, from market movements to expectations.
31. The copy of *Booms and Depressions* in the Bank's library was a personal gift from Irving Fisher to Montagu Norman, the famous Governor. Did he ever read it?
32. Discussed in more detail in Pepper (1990a: Ch. 7).
33. One of the features of the debate was failure of communication. In spite of being a joint chairman of the Church House conference, Fforde was to write in 1982:

    > The argument in favour of monetary base control did not in the end prevail. Perhaps this was because by the autumn of 1980 ... the need to have regard to a range of indicators, including the exchange rate, when judging the appropriateness of policy in respect of ultimate objectives, was becoming very evident. The behaviour of the target aggregate itself [sterling M3] did not seem to be giving a reliable signal. Monetary base control did not seem relevant to this problem. (Fforde 1983: 207)

    Fforde was correct to argue that sterling M3 was misleading, as described earlier in this book, but he failed to focus on the fact that the growth of the monetary base in real terms had collapsed: during the twelve months to mid

December 1980 it declined by 8 per cent in real terms. In the second half of the 1980 the monetary base and the exchange rate were giving the same message. The advocates of MBC had not managed to communicate this to the Bank.

34. Coin is a liability of the Treasury.
35. The operational details are described in Pepper (1990a: 58–60).
36. This is one of Congdon's criticisms of MBC.
37. Federal Reserve of St Louis data.
38. The attitude of some officials in the Treasury and the Bank to monetary targets may have been somewhat similar. By the middle of the 1980s, the secular trend of rising inflation in the UK had clearly been broken. They may have considered that monetary targets had done their work, were no longer needed and welcomed the opportunity to scrap them.
39. In a letter to the authors.
40. In a letter from an ex-senior official of the Bank to the authors.
41. Patrick Minford is one of the economists who argue in this way.
42. With interest rates very low the prices of fixed-rate bonds will be very high. The prices of such bonds will fall as debt deflation is cured. Banks may accordingly consider the risk in purchasing such assets is unacceptably high. Andrew Smithers (see, for example, Smithers 1999) has pointed out that the same argument does not apply to floating-rate bonds, which, he argues, should be issued to replace fixed-rate bonds.
43. This is somewhat similar to Recommendation 8.22 of the *Final Report* (published in April 2000) of the Bank of England Commission, established by the Conservative Party to review the establishment of the Monetary Policy Committee of the Bank.

    > Although the existing legislation permits action to be taken by the Chancellor in the event of a monetary crisis, there is currently no clear policy to deal with such circumstances. We believe that it would be appropriate, under circumstances of systemic shock for the Chancellor to set and publish not merely a revised target range, but a path of the targets and ranges leading back towards low inflation at a speed which he judges compatible with general economic objectives.

44. Retail M1 was an unofficial aggregate. It consisted of M1 less large interest-bearing sight deposits, which were an erratic component fluctuating with over-night money rates.
45. The end of exchange controls in the UK in October 1979 and the globalization of security markets had a long-lasting and fundamental effect on the behaviour of the monetary aggregates in the UK and other countries. Countries became far more exposed to international influences, particularly

events in the US. Monetary analysis had to be carried out allowing for global influences, which is much too large a subject for this book.

46. The 1981 Niehans report concluded that M0 rather than sterling M3 should be used as the main monetary measure. Niehans thought that monetary policy was too tight and should quickly be loosened.
47. For econometric support for the role of M0 as a leading indicator see Matthews and Ionnidis (1997).
48. In more detail, the usual result of a bank purchasing gilt-edged stock is a fall in the Treasury bill issue and no change in the total of banks' combined holdings of Treasury bills and gilt-edged stock. The total will, however, fall if gilt-edged prices rise as a result of the bank's purchase and this encourages a non-bank to sell stock, in which case the Treasury bill issue and banks' holdings of bills will not fall and banks will have increased their lending to the government.
49. There are, however, some indirect effects. Relative interest rates will change as banks bid more or less aggressively for funds, and this may alter non-banks' desire to hold public sector assets and the government's residual borrowing from banks and hence the money stock.

References

Bagehot, W. (1873), *Lombard Street: a Description of the Money Market* (ed. F. Genovese), Homewood, IL: Richard Irwin, 1962.

Bank of England (1984), 'Funding the Public Sector Borrowing Requirement: 1952–83', *Bank of England Quarterly Bulletin*, Vol. 24, No. 4, pp. 482–92.

Bank of England (1998), *Statistical Abstract 1998*, Part II, London: Bank of England.

Bank of England and HM Treasury (1980), *Monetary Control*, Cmnd. 7858, London: HMSO.

Bank of England Commission (2000), *Final Report*, London: Conservative Party.

Chancellor, E. (1999), *Devil Take the Hindmost: A History of Financial Speculation*, London: Macmillan.

Clarke, P. (1999), 'The Rise and Fall of Thatcherism', *Historical Research*, Vol. 72, No. 179, pp. 301–22.

Congdon, T. (1981), *Messel's Weekly Gilt Monitor*, 2 January.

Congdon, T. (1992), *Reflections on Monetarism*, London: Edward Elgar and Institute of Economic Affairs.

Congdon, T. (2000), *Monthly Economic Review*, Lombard Street Research, February.

Conservative Central Office (1976), *The Right Approach: A Statement Of Conservative Aims*, London: Conservative Party.

Dell, E. (1996), *The Chancellors*, London: HarperCollins.

Deutsche Bundesbank (1990), *Monthly Report*, March.

Dimsdale, N. H. (1991), 'British Monetary Policy since 1945', in Crafts, N. F. R. and Woodward, N. W. C. (eds), *The British Economy Since 1945*, Oxford: Oxford University Press.

Fforde, J. (1983), 'Setting Monetary Objectives', *Bank of England Quarterly Bulletin*, Vol. 23, No. 2, pp. 200–208.

Fisher, I. (1933), *Booms and Depressions: Some First Principles*, London: George Allen and Unwin.

Foot, M. D.K.W., Goodhart, C.A.E. and Hotson, A.C. (1979), 'Monetary base Control', *Bank of England Quarterly Bulletin*, Vol. 19, No. 2, pp. 149–56.

Friedman, M. (1962), 'Should There Be an Independent Monetary Authority?', in Yeager, L.B. (ed.), *In Search of A Monetary Constitution*, Cambridge, MA: Harvard University Press.

Friedman, M. (1980), 'Response to Questionnaire on Monetary Policy', in Treasury and Civil Service Committee, *Memoranda on Monetary Policy*, HC 720-I, London: HMSO.

Friedman, M. and Schwartz, A.J. (1982), *Monetary Trends in the United States and United Kingdom*, Chicago, IL: University of Chicago Press.

Friedman, M. and Schwartz, A.J. (1991), 'Alternative Approaches to Analysing Economic Data', *American Economic Review*, Vol. 81, No. 1, pp. 30–49.

Greenwell (1976), *Monetary Bulletin*, No. 54, June.

Greenwell (1980), *Monetary Bulletin*, No. 105, May.

Greenwell (1981), *Monetary Bulletin*, No. 114, January.

Hall, P.A. (1993), 'Policy Paradigms, Social Learning, and the State: The Case of Economic Policymaking in Britain', *Comparative Politics*, Vol. 25, No. 3, pp. 275–96.

Healey, D. (1989), *The Time of My Life*, London: Michael Joseph.

Healey, N. M. (1987), 'The UK 1979–82 "Monetarist Experiment": Why Economists Still Disagree', *Banca Nazionale del Lavoro Quarterly Review*, Vol. 40, No. 4, pp. 471–99.

Hendry, D. and Ericsson, N. R. (1983), 'Assertion Without Empirical Basis: an Econometric Appraisal of *Monetary Trends in the United States and the United Kingdom*, by Milton Friedman and Anna Schwartz', *Bank of England Panel of Economic Consultants*, Monetary Trends in the United Kingdom, Panel Paper No. 22, October, pp. 45–101.

Hendry, D. and Ericsson, N. R. (1991), 'An Econometric Analysis of UK Money Demand in *Monetary Trends in the United States and the United Kingdom* by Milton Friedman and Anna J. Schwartz', *American Economic Review*, Vol. 81, No. 1, pp. 8–38.

HM Treasury (1959), *Committee on the Working of the Monetary System, Report* (Radcliffe Committee), Cmd. 827, London: HMSO.

HM Treasury (1980), *Financial Statement and Budget Report 1980–81*, HC 500, London: HMSO.

HM Treasury (2000), *1999/2000 Debt Management Report*, London: HMSO.

Holly, S. and Longbottom, A. (1985), 'Monetary Trends in the UK: A Reappraisal of the Demand for Money', *London Business School Discussion Paper*, No. 147.

Howe, G. (1994), *Conflict of Loyalty*, London: Macmillan.

Howe, G., *et al.* (1977), *The Right Approach To The Economy: Outline Of An Economic Strategy For The Next Conservative Government*, London: Conservative Party.

Joseph, K. (1977), *Reversing the Trend*, London: Centre for Policy Studies.

Kindleberger, C.P. (1989), *Manias, Panics, and Crashes: A History of Financial Crises*, 2nd edn, London: Macmillan.

Laidler, D. and Parkin, M.J. (1975), 'Inflation – a Survey', *Economic Journal*, Vol. 85, pp. 741–809.

Lawson, N. (1978), 'The Economic Perils of Thinking for the Moment', *The Times*, 14 September.

Lawson, N. (1992), *The View From No. 11*, London: Bantam Press.

Leslie, D. (1993), *Advanced Macroeconomics: Beyond IS/LM*, Maidenhead: McGraw-Hill.

Matthews, K. and Ioannidis, C. (1997), 'Inflation: Too Much Money or Too Much Credit?', *Manchester School*, Vol. 65, No. 4, pp. 411–26.

Matthews, K. and Minford, A.P.L. (1987), 'Mrs Thatcher's Economic Policies 1979–87', *Economic Policy*, Vol. 2, No. 5, pp. 59–101.

Middleton, P. (1989), 'Economic Policy Formulation in the Treasury in the Post-War Period', *National Institute Economic Review*, No. 127, pp. 46–51.

Middleton, R. (1998), *Charlatans or Saviours? Economists and the British Economy from Marshall to Meade*, Cheltenham: Edward Elgar.

Middleton, R. (2000), *The British Economy Since 1945: Engaging With The Debate*, London: Macmillan.

Mishkin, F. (1997), *The Economics of Money, Banking and Financial Markets*, 5th edn, New York: Addison Wesley Longman.

Niehans, J. (1981), *The Appreciation of Sterling – Causes, Effects, Policies*, New York: Centre for Research in Government Policy and Business.

Oliver, M.J. (1997), *Whatever Happened To Monetarism? Economic Policy-making and Social Learning in the United Kingdom Since 1979*, Aldershot and Brookfield, VT: Ashgate Publishing Ltd.

Pepper, G.T. (1989), *A Firm Foundation For Monetary Policy*, Inquiry No. 8, London: IEA.

Pepper, G.T. (1990a), *Money, Credit and Inflation*, Research Monograph 44, London: IEA.

Pepper, G.T. (1990b), 'Monetary Policy – A Post-mortem and Proposal', The Tenth Mais Lecture, 3 May, City University Business School.

Pepper, G.T. (1993), 'A Policy for Debt-deflation', *Economic Outlook*, London Business School, February.

Pepper, G.T. (1994), *Money, Credit and Asset Prices*, London: Macmillan.

Pepper, G.T. (1998), *Inside Thatcher's Monetarist Revolution*, London: Macmillan/IEA.

Plummer, A. (1989), *Forecasting Financial Markets – The Truth Behind Technical Analysis*, London: Kogan Page.

Poole, W. (1982), 'Federal Reserve Operating Procedures: A Survey and Evaluation of the Historical Record Since October 1979', *Journal of Money, Credit and Banking*, Vol. 14, No. 4, Part 2, pp. 575–96.

Sargent, T. (1993), *Rational Expectations and Inflation*, 2nd edn, New York: HarperCollins.

Smithers, A. (1999), 'The Debate over Japan's Monetary Policy', *World Market Update*, London: Smithers & Co. Ltd.

Thatcher, M. (1993), *The Downing Street Years*, London: HarperCollins.

Thatcher, M. (1995), *The Path To Power*, London: HarperCollins.

Treasury and Civil Service Committee (1980), *Monetary Control* (two volumes), 3rd Report, HC 713-I and HC 713-II, London: HMSO.

Viner, J. (1932), 'International Aspects of the Gold Standard', in Wright, Q. (ed.), *Gold and Monetary Stabilization: Lectures on the Harris Foundation*, Chicago, IL: University of Chicago Press.

Walters, A. (1984), 'The United Kingdom: Political Economy and Macroeconomics', in Brunner, K. and Meltzer, A. (eds), *Carnegie-Rochester Conference Series on Public Policy*, Vol. 21, pp. 259–80.

Walters, A. (1986), *Britain's Economic Renaissance*, Oxford: Oxford University Press.

Walters, A. (1988), 'Money on a Roller-Coaster', *The Independent*, 14 July.

Wass, D. (1978), 'The Changing Problems of Economic Management', *Economic Trends*, No. 293.

Wood, G.E. (1995), 'The Quantity Theory in the 1980s', in M. Blaug *et al.*, *The Quantity Theory of Money from Locke to Keynes and Friedman*, Aldershot: Edward Elgar.

Index